ISS

Dediu Newsletter

Author: Michael M. Dediu

Monthly news, reviews, comments and suggestions for a better and wiser world

---

Vol. 3, Nr. 2 (26), 6 January 2019

DERC Publishing House

Tewksbury (Boston), Massachusetts, U. S. A.

For subscriptions please use the contact form at www.derc.com

Published and printed in the
United States of America
On the Great Seal of the United States are included:
E Pluribus Unum (Out of many, one)
Annuit Coeptis (He has approved of the undertakings)
Novus Ordo Seclorum (New order of the ages)

Dediu, Michael M.

Dediu Newsletter Vol 3, Number 2 (26), 6 January 2019
Monthly reviews, comments and suggestions for a better and
wiser world

ISSN 2475-2061
ISBN 978-1-939757-82-1

Preface

Happy and Healthy New Year 2019!

December 2018 was full of events, like partially closing the U.S. government, but also good events: Oregon State University engineers are using 3D animations techniques to increase the precision of radiation therapy for prostate cancer, so that neighboring healthy tissues and organs are not affected; Amazon is testing its cashier-less checkout technology for bigger stores, sources tell the WSJ; a successful rocket launch on Monday, 3 Dec, by SpaceX marked twin milestones for the company's drive to ease access for commercial satellites into orbit - the mission was SpaceX's 19th launch this year, topping its previous record of 18 in 2017; the Falcon 9 rocket also carried the largest number of satellites - a cluster of more than five dozen - ever stacked on top a U.S. booster.

In this 2nd newsletter of the third volume, the 26th in total, we included the most relevant news, in a balanced approach, usually directly from the source, to help the general public better understand the realities around us. We included also several nice photos - I thank my wife for her photo assistance. Being well and correctly informed is a sine qua non requirement for everybody, in order to make the right decisions for the future.

Enjoy this newsletter and be optimist!

Michael M. Dediu, Ph. D.

Tewksbury (Boston), U. S. A., 6 January 2019

Italia, Venezia, on Riva degli Schiavoni, about 300 m east from Piazza San Marco, Londra Palace Hotel (left), Monumento a Vittorio Emanuele II (back, Monument to King Victor Emanuel II). There is heavy foot traffic on this Riva degli Schiavoni, being close to Piazza San Marco, to the vaporetto stops, and having a gorgeous view to the south: San Giorgio Maggiore Island, and Giudecca.

Table of Contents

New York, 27 Nov 2007: West 42nd Street near 7th Avenue and Times Square, with many tall buildings around, like the Conde Nast Building (1996-1999, 264 m, 48-story office tower, on the left).

United States of America

(Population 324.4 M, rank 3, growth 0.7%. Free: 89 of 100. Area 9.52 M km^2, rank 4.).

Reports: A recent study showed that only 1 in 4 Americans (25%) can name all three branches of government.

Reports: The U.S. national debt is over $21.25 T (about 10,000 times bigger than 118 years ago, in 1900), and each family share of this debt is over $956.9 K.

Reports: The 30th U.S. President Calvin Coolidge (4 July 1872, Vermont – 5 January 1933, Northampton, Mass, aged 60.5, President for 5.7 years: 2 Aug 1923 (age 51) – 4 March 1929 (age 56.7)). During his presidency, the national US debt decreased by 5.41 B (24.21%), from $22.34 B to $16.93 B (this $16.93 B is 0.07% of the current debt). If this US debt decrease would have continued in the same way, in 1946 the US would have had a national surplus – instead the US national debt in 1946 was $269.286 B (1590.58% increase = 15.9 times bigger than in 1929). About 90 years ago, in 1928, President Coolidge said, "It is much more important to kill bad bills than to pass good ones". In November 2018 Republicans lost the House because they failed to deliver on their campaign promise to cut spending. While Republicans were successful in passing tax cuts, they failed to cut spending in any way, despite the fact that they were holding a majority in the House and Senate. For all their talk of spending cuts on the campaign trail, Republicans have been asleep at the wheel in Washington.

History: Wednesday, Dec. 5, marked the 85th anniversary of Prohibition being officially repealed, in 1933, ending the U.S.'s failed experiment in banning alcohol. Many think that the U.S. alcohol markets have operated free and clear in the decades since Prohibition, but sadly the reality is far more complex. Across the country, all levels of government continue to have woefully outdated and restrictive laws on their books concerning alcohol.

Worst of all, many of these laws do little to protect public health and safety, but rather operate mainly to help vested economic interests.

Reports: In 2000, at the groundbreaking for a minor league baseball stadium in Camden, New Jersey, then-Governor of New Jersey said "The state's economic development authorities, had "heard the message from the movie, Field of Dreams: 'If you build it, they will come.'" Taxpayers spent more than $18 M to build the stadium that would eventually be named Campbell's Field, as part of a minor league ballpark-building frenzy across New Jersey, that saw similar stadiums erected in Newark, Atlantic City, and Somerset—all part of redevelopment schemes that attracted independent minor league teams (that is, minor league teams not affiliated with the Major League Baseball farm system). Less than two decades later, taxpayers in New Jersey will pay another $1 M to tear down Campbell's Field.

.   Reports: U.S. health spending hits $3.5 T but growth slows.

Reports: The U.S. budget deficit in the first two months of fiscal 2019, which began Oct. 1, was $13 B, or 6% higher than the previous year, according to the Congressional Budget Office. The federal debt and deficit have grown dramatically since President Trump took office, a product of military spending, tax cuts, bipartisan spending, and ongoing growth in mandatory programs like Social Security and Medicare.

Reports: Americans trust their state governments to handle issues as important as education and health care, and pay them more than a trillion dollars in taxes annually, yet people know very little about these institutions. – Johns Hopkins University

Reports: An analysis from Indiana University researchers has found that half the people pursuing scientific careers at institutions of higher education will depart the field after five years -- a sharp contrast compared to 50 years ago.

20 December 2018. Reports: The Senate has passed a bill to overhaul criminal sentencing guidelines in an 87-12 vote. The

measure would curtail jail sentences for some nonviolent offenders, help ex-convicts adjust to life after release, and address disparities between crack and powder cocaine offenses. Judges would also get more discretion to set sentences for people charged with low-level drug crimes who cooperate with police.

The United States surpasses other nations around the globe in healthcare costs, a recent study found. Notably, the average cost of an outpatient visit in the U.S. in 2016 (in 2017 international dollars [I\$]) was I\$476. Only one nation—Switzerland—was higher, at I\$502.

Over 155 people permanently leave Chicago daily.

Millions of comments about the FCC's Net Neutrality Rules were fake. Now the Feds are investigating.

Since 2008, the average monthly per-line subscription cost of a wireless plan has declined, but the share of taxes for an average bill has grown from 15.1% to a record 19.1%, according to new Tax Foundation research. While rates can vary, most states impose higher taxes and fees on mobile phone plans than other goods and services.

83% of U.S. homes have Internet, same as in 2013.

Puerto Rico: (Population 3.6 M, rank 134, decrease 0.1%; an unincorporated territory of the United States, located in the northeast Caribbean Sea, 1,600 km southeast of Miami, Florida.).

United Nations.   There are 195 officially recognized countries. Around 44,000 people work for the United Nations. There is a wide range of jobs: Researchers, IT-specialists, lawyers, experts on finance and administration, or translators work at the New York headquarters, at the official locations, or at specialized agencies. More than half of the UN's workforce is employed in the field, in projects of humanitarian aid, or on peace missions.
Reports: The future of the World Trade Organization is in focus, as a meeting of the general council convenes, against the

backdrop of ongoing trade wars. The U.S. has said it wouldn't agree with the selection process, to replace retiring judges on the Appellate Body, until broader issues with the WTO's dispute resolution system had been settled, creating uncertainty in the global trade watchdog.

USA, Boston (founded in 1630): tall ships from many countries, at the Boston Fish Pier (opened in 1915).

China, Japan, and neighbors

China: (Population 1.4 B, rank 1, growth 0.4%. Freedom House reports for 2018: Not Free (15 of 100). Area 9.59 M km², rank 3). Reports: China's trade surplus with the U.S. jumped in November, widening to a record $35.5 B.

10 December 2018. Reports: After warning Ottawa of "severe consequences," China's foreign ministry called in the U.S. ambassador on Sunday, 9 Dec, to lodge a "strong protest" over the arrest of Huawei CFO Meng Wanzhou in Vancouver, and said the U.S. should withdraw its arrest warrant.

12 December 2018. Reports: More fingers are being pointed at China for last month's massive breach at Marriott, that compromised the data of 500 M Starwood users. The New York Times is the latest to suggest the intrusion was part of a larger state-sponsored intelligence gathering effort. "China firmly opposes all forms of cyberattack, and cracks down on it in accordance with the law," said Geng Shuang, a spokesman for China's Ministry of Foreign Affairs.

Reports: Traditional Chinese culture, which is profoundly optimistic regarding the world, and has deep spiritual roots, was displaced by Communism in China. Many organizations, like the New York-based Shen Yun, are keeping this precious heritage alive.

BEIJING, Dec. 12 (Xinhua) -- President Xi Jinping reiterated on Wednesday, 12 Dec, that China will adhere to the path of multilateralism, and open its door wider to the world.

Xi made the remarks when meeting with foreign delegates attending the just concluded 2018 Imperial Springs International Forum, held in Guangzhou, south China's Guangdong Province.

He briefed the delegates on achievements of China's reform and opening-up during the past 40 years, and important measures of a new round of opening-up at a higher level, expounded on China's relations with the world, and listened to the delegates' remarks.

Xi said this year's Imperial Springs International Forum coincides with the 40th anniversary of China's reform and opening-up.

The forum, held on Dec. 10 in southern China's Guangzhou, gathered some 200 former world leaders, renowned scholars and business elites to discuss the theme of advancing reform and opening-up, promoting win-win cooperation. "The past 40 years have witnessed tremendous achievements in China's development, and remarkable improvement of people's livelihood, from shortage to abundance, from poverty to moderate prosperity," Xi said.

China's reform and opening-up drive is people-oriented, Xi stressed, adding that a distinctive feature of the country's economy in the new era is the shift from rapid growth to high-quality development, from quantitative expansion to qualitative growth.

"For more balanced and full development, we must further deepen reform and expand opening-up," said the Chinese president.

During the Boao Forum for Asia annual conference in April, Xi announced a series of measures to expand the country's opening-up, including substantially easing market access, creating a more attractive investment environment, strengthening intellectual property protection, and actively expanding imports. At the opening ceremony of the first China International Import Expo in Shanghai, Xi announced new measures to further expand opening-up.

"China will adhere to the path of multilateralism, and open the door wider to the world," Xi said.

Saying China's economy has maintained overall stability and steady progress, Xi noted that the goal of "making people well-off" pushes the important potential for the country to achieve further growth.

With the increasing income, Chinese people's pursuit of a high-quality life will bring about greater consumer demand, Xi said. "We are firmly confident in the long-term positive fundamentals of China's economic development, as well as in the mid- to high-speed economic growth bringing the economy to a medium-to-high level."

Noting that China's role as an active defender and contributor to international rules has been acknowledged by the international community, Xi said China's reform and opening-up is all-round, and the country's development is an opportunity for the whole world.

"The practice of China's reform and opening-up has fully proven that only by win-win cooperation can a country achieve long-term development," he said.

Xi stressed that the Belt and Road Initiative, which originates from China and belongs to the world, is aimed at building a new platform for win-win cooperation for the international community.

He reiterates the principle of extensive consultation, joint contribution and shared benefits in promoting cooperation under the Belt and Road Initiative.

"China's overseas investment and cooperation in capacity building and infrastructure construction have driven industrialization of the countries concerned, and promoted local people's livelihood and economic and social development," said Xi. Xi said the Chinese side sincerely hopes that all countries will join the Belt and Road partnership, and deliver more benefits for all people.

He said China's efforts to promote and build a new type of international relations and a community with a shared future for humanity are also aimed at achieving win-win cooperation among all countries. Noting that China's reform and opening-up has left a glorious chapter in history, Xi said the policy will also enable China to score new achievements in the next 40 years that will deeply impress the world. The foreign delegates, including former Latvian President Vaira Vike-Freiberga, said that China's reform and opening-up have brought about tremendous changes in China, and had a major positive impact on the world.

They advocated developing inter-state ties on the basis of enhancing mutual trust and win-win cooperation, urging all sides to maintain world peace, promote common growth, and oppose unilateralism, isolationism and protectionism.

The foreign delegates also praised the Belt and Road Initiative, saying it yielded tangible benefits for many countries.

Reports: The official Chinese website about President Xi gives info and links to all kinds of crimes and other similar staff, completely unrelated to Xi – does he know and approve this very bad activity on his website?

14 December 2018. Xinhua. Xi Jinping, general secretary of the Communist Party of China (CPC) Central Committee, presided over a meeting of the committee's Political Bureau Thursday, 13 Dec, which studied the economic work for 2019, and made plans for building good conduct and political integrity within the CPC, as well as fighting corruption. Members of the Political Bureau heard a work report from the Central Commission for Discipline Inspection (CCDI) of the CPC at the meeting.

In 2018, China maintained sustained, healthy development of its economy and stability in social order amid a complicated international environment, and the arduous tasks involved with domestic reform, development, and stability, according to a statement released after the meeting. The People's Republic of China (PRC) will mark its 70th founding anniversary in 2019, a pivotal year for securing a decisive victory in finishing the building of a moderately prosperous society in all respects, the statement said.

Next year, the country should uphold the underlying principle of pursuing progress while ensuring stability, adhere to the new development philosophy, and push forward high-quality development, it added.

China should continue to take pursuing supply-side structural reform as the main task, deepen market-oriented reform, expand opening up at a high level, and speed up the building of a modernized economy, according to the statement.

Efforts should also be continued to fight the "three tough battles" of controlling risks, reducing poverty and tackling pollution, stimulate the vitality of micro entities, and meanwhile innovate and improve macroeconomic regulation. To raise market confidence, the country will keep economic growth at a reasonable level, further stabilize employment, the financial market, foreign trade, foreign investment, domestic investment, and expectations, the statement said.

By maintaining continuous and healthy economic growth and overall social stability, the country will "lay the decisive foundation for finishing the building of a moderately prosperous society in all respects, and celebrate the 70th anniversary of the founding of the PRC with excellent results," the statement said.

The meeting stressed that changes in the international environment and domestic conditions should be looked at dialectically, urging the Party to be prepared for potential adversities.

The country should continue to seize the important period of strategic opportunity for development and manage its own affairs with firm confidence and initiative, according to the meeting.

It demanded strategic resolve, solid efforts, better coordination, a focus on major contradictions, and well-managed rhythm and intensity, to seek an optimal policy mix and maximum effects.

The statement said efforts should be continued next year to fight the "three tough battles."

It also called for moves to advance high-quality development of the manufacturing sector, cultivate the strength of the domestic market, push forward rural vitalization strategy, advance regional coordinated development, speed up economic reforms and all-around opening up, and improve people's wellbeing.

It is a must for the Party to improve its ability to lead economic work, according to the statement. Since the 19th CPC National Congress, a sweeping victory has been won in the fight against corruption and major outcomes achieved in exercising full and strict governance over the Party, said the statement.

However, the anti-corruption fight remains grave and complex, and the strict governance over the Party remains a long and arduous task, the meeting noted, stressing strict discipline must be adhered to on a long-term basis. Action should be taken to fight the practice of formalities for formalities' sake and bureaucratism, and ensure the implementation of the major decisions and plans of the CPC Central Committee, said the statement.

The meeting called for efforts to develop new systems and mechanisms for disciplinary inspection and supervision, make groundbreaking innovations in regular and long-term supervision, and address the corruption that occurs on the people's doorsteps.

Xi was briefed on the work of the CCDI for 2018 and preparations for the upcoming third plenary session of the 19th CCDI of the CPC, which is scheduled for January 11 to 13, 2019.

15 December 2018. Xinhua. Xi Jinping, general secretary of the Communist Party of China (CPC) Central Committee, stressed consistent efforts to reform the national supervisory system, and improve law-based and procedure-based anti-graft work.

Xi made the statement at a group study session of the CPC Central Committee Political Bureau held Thursday13 Dec, afternoon.

The reform on the Party's disciplinary inspection system should be carried out together with the reform of the national supervisory system, so that the enforcement of Party disciplines and laws are linked, and effectively coordinated, with the judicial system, he said.

Noting that the reform on the national supervisory system has made important progress, Xi said measures should be made to strengthen deterrence, so officials don't dare to, strengthen the cage of institutions, so they're unable to, and strengthen their vigilance, so they have no desire to commit acts of corruption. Xi highlighted that the goal of the reform is to strengthen supervision over public power, and everyone in the public service. He demanded law-based use of public power, closing supervision loopholes, and minimizing the space where power can be exercised at will.

Action should be taken to curb cases of abuse of power and dereliction of duty, Xi said, urging efforts to support officials who are willing to assume responsibility, and clear the names for those suffering from false accusations, or are framed in a timely manner.

Xi spoke of the need to maintain a tough stance on corruption, guide cadres to strengthen their ideals and convictions, tighten political supervision, improve related laws and rules, enhance coordination and strengthen the leadership of Party committees at all levels over the disciplinary inspection and supervisory system reforms.

The disciplinary inspection and supervisory agencies should leverage the advantage of working together to better coordinate their respective oversight functions, Xi said.

He noted that the disciplinary inspection and supervisory agencies must closely follow the CPC Central Committee regarding their thinking, political orientation, and actions.

Xi urged staff of the disciplinary inspection and supervisory agencies to enhance their sense of laws and rules, especially the awareness of following due procedures, and to set an example to observe the laws and disciplines.

17 December 2018. Xinhua. President Xi Jinping sent a congratulatory letter to the 3rd Understanding China Conference which opened in Beijing on Sunday, 16 Dec. Yang Jiechi, a member of the Political Bureau of the Communist Party of China (CPC) Central Committee, read the letter at the opening ceremony.

The world today faces unprecedented changes in a century, peace and development is still the theme of the times, and meanwhile, the humanity is facing many common challenges, Xi said in the letter.

China is willing to work with other countries to actively promote the building of a new type of international relations featuring mutual respect, fairness and justice, and win-win cooperation, and to facilitate the construction of a community with a shared future for humanity, thus making new greater contributions to world peace and development, Xi said. Xi stressed that this year marks the 40th anniversary of China's reform and opening up, which has written a glorious chapter in China's development, with China's relations with the world becoming closer and closer.

China will continue to comprehensively deepen reform and expand opening up, remain committed to the new development philosophy, push forward the supply-side structural reform, and take coordinated efforts to stabilize growth, propel reform, make structural adjustments, improve people's livelihoods and guard against risks, so as to promote high-quality development of the country's economy and offer more cooperation opportunities to the world, Xi said.

He expressed the hope that the conference participants can have in-depth discussions and gather consensus to enhance their understanding of China, and also help the world better understand China, thus promoting the exchanges and cooperation between China and the world, to achieve common development and prosperity. Yang, also director of the Office of the Foreign Affairs Commission of the CPC Central Committee, delivered a speech at the opening ceremony.

He said that with its own constant development, China will continue to provide a stable cornerstone for world peace and development, inject inexhaustible impetus into global economic growth, build important platforms for win-win cooperation among different countries, set an example for eliminating poverty and backwardness, contribute oriental wisdom to solving hotspot issues, and provide firm support for safeguarding international order.

Nearly 600 people will attend the conference, including about 40 famous global politicians, strategists and entrepreneurs.

18 December 2018. Reports: "No one is in a position to dictate to the Chinese people what should or should not be done," President Xi Jinping said in an address commemorating the 40th anniversary of the opening up of the Chinese economy. While he didn't mention trade tensions, he touched on the rapid growth of coastal cities, joining the WTO, the Belt and Road initiative, establishment of free trade zones, and the country's first import expo.

18 December 2018. Reports: China cut its holdings of U.S. Treasuries - by $12.5B in October - for a fifth consecutive month, amid a broader decline in foreign demand for U.S. government debt due to a strong dollar. Beijing's Treasury appetite has garnered attention due to its continued trade dispute with Washington, which has contributed to the renminbi falling toward the RMB7 threshold vs. the greenback, for the first time since the financial crisis.

Reports: BEIJING, China - The Civil Aviation Administration of China (CAAC) reported that the Asian nation aims to build 216 new airports in the country by 2035. CAAC noted that China currently has 234 civil airports, and plans to have approximately 450 by 2035, according to a report from the state-run China Daily.

20 December 2018. Reuters: IBM and HPE are victims of Chinese cyberattacks.

Reports: Two of China's biggest network equipment manufacturers may soon be barred from the U.S. market. The U.S. administration is considering an executive order that would ban American companies from using gear made by China's Huawei and ZTE, sources told Reuters. The U.S. alleges the companies work at the behest of the Chinese government, and their equipment could be used to spy on Americans.

20 December 2018. Reports: The US indicted two Chinese men accused of hacking into computer networks of Western companies and government agencies, and accused Beijing of cyber-spying. UK Foreign Secretary Jeremy Hunt described the men's actions as "one of the most significant and widespread cyber intrusions against the UK and allies uncovered to date".
The Foreign Office said hackers, acting on behalf of the Chinese Ministry of State Security, were stealing commercial secrets from firms in Europe, Asia and the US.
Officials said their activities were so extensive, they were "putting at risk" economic growth in the UK, and the wider global economy.

28 December 2018. Reports: A third prototype of China's home-built C919 passenger jet completed its first test flight today, with the goal of obtaining certification from Chinese and European regulators by the end of 2020. China's first national passenger jet aims to challenge the dominance of Boeing's 737 and Airbus's A320, bringing the Asian nation a step closer to its goal of becoming a global civil aerospace player.

31 December 2018. Reports: President Trump said he had a "very good call" on trade with China's Xi Jinping on Saturday, 29 December, claiming that "big progress" was being made on this front, while the latter said both sides wanted "stable progress."

1 January 2019. Xinhua. Chinese President Xi Jinping and U.S. President Donald Trump on Tuesday, 1 Jan, exchanged

congratulations on the 40th anniversary of the establishment of China-U.S. diplomatic relations. In his congratulatory message, Xi said China-U.S. relations have experienced ups and downs, and made historic progress over the past 40 years, bringing huge benefits to the two peoples, and contributing greatly to world peace, stability and prosperity. History has proved that cooperation is the best choice for both sides, Xi said.

Currently, China-U.S. relations are in an important stage, he noted. "I attach great importance to the development of China-U.S. relations and am willing to work with President Trump to summarize the experience of the development of China-U.S. relations, and implement the consensus we have reached in a joint effort to advance China-U.S. relations featuring coordination, cooperation and stability, so as to better benefit the two peoples as well as the people of the rest of the world," Xi said.

For his part, Trump said Jan. 1, 2019 marks the 40th anniversary of the establishment of U.S.-China diplomatic relations.

Great progress has been made in the development of bilateral ties over the past years, he noted. Trump said it is his priority to promote cooperative and constructive U.S.-China relations, adding that his solid friendship with President Xi has laid a firm foundation for the great achievements of the two countries in coming years.

1 January 2019. Xinhua. President Xi Jinping delivered a New Year speech Monday, 31 Dec 2018, evening, calling on the whole nation to strive for "an unprecedented and great cause" in the year 2019, the 70th anniversary of the founding of the People's Republic of China. Chinese people, who are self-reliant, hardworking and enterprising, have created a China miracle recognized by the world, he said, vowing to rely on the people and push forward the cause step by step.

"In 2018, we had a fulfilling and focused year," Xi said in the speech, summarizing the progress made in 2018, which saw the country's economy stay "within a reasonable range."

The campaign to prevent and control pollution of air, water and soil went smoothly while the people's wellbeing and their living standards improved, he said.

National strategies including the coordinated development of the Beijing-Tianjin-Hebei region, the development of Yangtze

Economic Belt, and the construction of Guangdong-Hong Kong-Macao Greater Bay Area were steadily implemented.

Xi also mentioned the achievements he witnessed during his inspection trips: the improved ecology along the Yangtze River, the agricultural harvest in northeast provinces, the reform and vitality in Shenzhen and Shanghai, as well as the opening of the Hong Kong-Zhuhai-Macao Bridge. China launched Chang'e-4 lunar probe, conducted sea trials of its second aircraft carrier, completed first water takeoff of its independently-developed large amphibious aircraft, and took solid steps in BeiDou Navigation Satellite System's global service, Xi noted in the speech.

Around 10 millions of people in the country's rural areas were lifted out of poverty in 2018, said the president, recollecting his visits to villages in Sichuan, Shandong, Liaoning and Guangdong provinces.

In the year marking the 40th anniversary of the country's reform and opening-up, China unveiled a systematic, comprehensive and restructuring reform of both Party and State institutions. More than 100 important reform measures were rolled out, he said. "China's reforms will never stop and its door will only open even wider."

Joint efforts are needed as China faces both opportunities and challenges in 2019, Xi noted.

In the new year, Xi said, the policies to cut taxes and fees should be well implemented to ease the burden on enterprises.

Sincere appreciation should be given to professionals in all areas while efforts be made to motivate responsible and competent grass-roots officials, he said. The goal of lifting 10 million rural residents above the poverty line should be fulfilled as planned, he said, adding that veterans should receive proper attention and care.

Xi also extended gratitude to millions of hardworking people, such as deliverymen, sanitation workers and taxi drivers.

In 2018, China hosted diplomatic events including the annual Boao Forum for Asia, the Shanghai Cooperation Organization Qingdao summit, and the Beijing summit of the Forum on China-Africa Cooperation. China put forward its proposals and made its voice heard, and enlarged its circle of friends in 2018, Xi said. In a world that is undergoing changes unseen in a century, China will remain confident and resolute in safeguarding its sovereignty and security, and maintain its sincerity and goodwill for safeguarding world peace and promoting common prosperity, he said.

China will actively promote the joint construction of the Belt and Road, continue to promote the building of a community with a shared future for humanity, and work relentlessly for an even more prosperous and beautiful world, he said.

Hong Kong. (Population 7.3 M, rank 104, growth 0.8%. Partly Free: 61 of 100).
21 December 2018. Reports: A flurry of IPOs in Hong Kong propelled the financial center to first place in volumes globally in 2018. Companies raised a total of $36.3 B, well ahead of New York Stock Exchange's $28.9 B, and a 174% increase year-on-year.

Macau (Population 622 K, rank 167, growth 1.7 %.)

Taiwan: (Population 23.6 M, rank 56, growth 0.3%. Free, 91 of 100). 2 January 2019. Reports: China reserves the right to use force to bring Taiwan under its control, President Xi Jinping told a gathering in Beijing, but will strive to achieve peaceful "reunification" with the self-ruled island.

Japan (Population 127.5 M, rank 11, decrease 0.2%. Free, 96 of 100). 3 December 2018. Reports: The future of the Renault-Nissan alliance "is up to private-sector shareholders, and it's important to maintain a stable relationship," Japanese Prime Minister Shinzo Abe told French President Emmanuel Macron at the G20 summit in Argentina. The French government holds a 15% stake in Renault, which in turn has a 43.4% holding in Nissan, and voting majority at its shareholder meetings. Nissan's reciprocal 15% Renault stake carries no voting rights.
Reports: A recent breakthrough in the design of medical device coaxial cables is expected to enable a new generation of small, flexible, and intelligent catheters according to Japanese wire and cable supplier Junkosha.
Reports: More companies are abandoning current and upcoming 5G gear from Huawei, like Japan's big three telecom operators, Kyodo News reports, amid fears that the equipment could contain "backdoors" for use by spies.
Reports: Japan's biggest-ever IPO - SoftBank has priced its domestic telecom business at ¥1,500 per share and will sell an extra

160 M shares to meet strong demand. That will raise ¥2.65 T ($23.6 B) and make the stock sale one of the largest of all time globally. Shares of the new entity, SoftBank Corp., will begin trading on the Tokyo Stock Exchange on Dec. 19.

Reports: Osaka University researchers have developed an AI-based system that has the potential to differentiate between different types of cancer cells. The research could have major implications in the field of oncology.

Reports: Japan's export growth slowed to a crawl in November, as shipments to the U.S. and China weakened sharply. The value of exports rose 0.1% from a year earlier, as the trade war weighed on the world's third-largest economy.

Afghanistan: (Population 35.5 M, rank 40, growth 2.5%. Not free: 24 of 100).

South Korea: (Population 50.9 M, rank 27, growth 0.4%. Free, 82 of 100).

North Korea: (Population 25.4 M, rank 52, growth 0.5%. Not free: 3 of 100). 2 January 2019. Reports: North Korea's Kim Jong-un said he's ready to meet President Trump anytime to denuclearize the Korean Peninsula, but warned he may have to take an alternative path if U.S. sanctions and pressure continue.

Vietnam (Population 95.5 M, rank 15, growth 1%. Not free, 20 of 100). 23 October 2018.

Laos (Population. 6.8 M, rank 106, growth 1.5%. Not free: 12 of 100).

Cambodia (Population 16 M, rank 71, growth 1.5%. Not Free 31 of 100).

Mongolia (Population 3 M, rank 137, growth 1.6%. Free 85 of 100)

Nepal: (Population 29.3 M, rank 48, growth 1.1%. Partly free 52 of 100).

Russia, Switzerland, Eastern Europe

Russia: (Population 143.9 M, rank 9, growth 0%. Not free: 20 of 100. Area 17 M km^2, rank 1) History: On 27 January 2020 it will be 200 years since the discovery of the Antarctica by Russian explorers Fabian Gottlieb von Bellingshausen and Mikhail Lazarev, in 1820.

11 December 2018 – 100th anniversary of the birth of Alexander Solzhenitsyn – a bronze monument, sitting on a granite pedestal, was unveiled in Moscow, in the presence of the Russian President.

20 December 2018. Reports: Aluminum prices sank to a 16-month low at $1,911 a ton after the U.S. Treasury said it would lift sanctions on the core empire of Russian businessman Oleg Deripaska, including aluminum giant Rusal and its parent En+.

1 January 2019. Xinhua. Chinese President Xi Jinping and Russian President Vladimir Putin exchanged New Year greetings on Monday, 31 Dec 2018. In his congratulatory message to Putin, Xi said that the year 2018 has a special significance in China-Russia relations, and both countries have smoothly completed their respective important domestic political agendas, and opened a new era for China-Russia ties. During the year, China and Russia witnessed more frequent high-level exchanges, deepened mutual political trust, and a series of achievements from bilateral pragmatic cooperation in various fields, Xi said.

The Year of China-Russia Local Cooperation and Exchange program proceeded smoothly in 2018, and the popular support for friendship from generation to generation between the two peoples has been further consolidated, the Chinese president said.

The two countries collaborated actively in international and regional affairs and played important constructive roles in safeguarding international fairness and justice, as well as world peace and stability, he said. The year 2019 marks the 70th anniversary of the establishment of diplomatic relations between China and Russia, Xi said, noting that he is willing to work with Putin to prompt bilateral relations and cooperation in various fields, to make new progress and bring more benefits to the two countries and peoples.

In his congratulatory message, Putin extended warm New Year greetings to Xi, and wished Chinese people happiness and good health.

In 2018, the Russia-China comprehensive strategic partnership of coordination reached an unprecedented level, with substantiated political dialogues and rapidly expanding two-way trade, Putin said.

The Year of China-Russia Local Cooperation and Exchange got off to a good start, and the two countries conducted fruitful cooperation to solve major global and regional issues, he said.

Russia and China will celebrate the 70th anniversary of the establishment of diplomatic ties in 2019, the Russian president said, voicing his belief that both sides will take the opportunity to continue effective cooperation in bilateral and multilateral affairs.

Also on Monday, Chinese Premier Li Keqiang and his Russian counterpart Dmitry Medvedev exchanged New Year greetings.

In his congratulatory message, Li said China would like to promote cooperation with Russia in trade, energy, finance, technology, agriculture, humanities and other areas to facilitate common development of both nations.

For his part, Medvedev said that Russia highly valued the achievements of the 23rd regular meeting between Chinese and Russian heads of governments, and is willing to work actively with China to promote bilateral cooperation in various fields.

Switzerland: (Population 8.4 M, rank 99, growth 0.9%. Free: 96 of 100). 7 December 2018. Reports: Switzerland's divided cabinet looks bound for a disagreement with the EU, following today's likely rejection of a draft treaty that has exposed deep divisions in Swiss attitudes toward its biggest trading partner EU. Brussels will likely ban EU-based banks and brokers from trading on Swiss stock exchanges beyond the end of 2018, as a punitive measure, should Bern not sign off on the deal. In turn, that would prompt Swiss retaliation.

13 December 2018. Reports: The Swiss National Bank kept its ultra-loose monetary policy in place, citing a delicate exchange-rate situation, weakening inflation, and international tensions as reasons to maintain its expansive course into a fourth year.

Reports: Switzerland leads 5th consecutive edition of IMD (Institute for Management Development) world talent ranking'

Reports: The European Commission is expected to officially give Switzerland a six-month reprieve that will allow its stock exchanges to maintain access to EU clients until June 2019. It had previously warned that the exchanges faced suspension in a row over a new treaty governing ties between Switzerland and the EU, which faces domestic criticism that it impinges too much on Swiss sovereignty.

Austria: (Population 8.7 M, rank 98, growth 0.3%. Free: 95 of 100). 28 December 2018. Reports: Royal Dutch Shell has officially said goodbye to New Zealand with the sale of its oil and gas assets to Austria's OMV for $578 M. The move is part of a drive to simplify its upstream portfolio and reshape the oil major. Shell's $30 B divestment program for 2016-18 included oil sands interests in Canada, onshore upstream operations in Gabon, as well as assets in the North Sea and Australia.

Finland, Helsinki Airport, located in Vantaa, 17 km north of Helsinki, built in 1952.

Poland: (Population 38.1 M, rank 37, decrease 0.1%. Free: 89 of 100).

Croatia: (Population 4.1 M, rank 129, decrease 0.6%. Free: 87 of 100).

Finland: (Population 5.5 M, rank 116, growth 0.4%. Free: 100 of 100). History: The important Conference on Security and Cooperation in Europe (CSCE) took place in Finlandia Hall of Helsinki, on 1 August 1975.

Romania (Population: 19.6 M, rank 59, decrease 0.5%. Free: 84 of 100) Reports: A Romania hospital reported 39 babies were diagnosed with a superbug. The Giulesti Maternity hospital was closed Nov. 30 due to the outbreak. The number of newborns now diagnosed is triple the figure released last month.
19 December 2018. Reports: Romania Giulesti Maternity hospital hit by superbug will reopen. The Giulesti Maternity hospital in Bucharest, where 45 babies were diagnosed with a drug-resistant superbug, has been given the all-clear to reopen.

Moldova: (Population: 4 M, rank 132, decrease 0.2%. Partly Free: 62 of 100).

Belarus: (Population: 9.4 M, rank 93, decrease 0.1%. Not Free: 20 of 100).

Bulgaria: (Population: 7 M, rank 105, decrease 0.7%. Free: 80 of 100).

Slovenia: (Population: 2 M, rank 148, growth 0.1%. Free: 92 of 100).

Hungary: (Population: 9.7 M, rank 91, decrease 0.3%. Free: 76 of 100)

Ukraine: (Population: 44.2 M, rank 32, decrease 0.5%. Partly free: 61 of 100).

Latvia: (Population: 1.9 M, rank 150, decrease 1.1%. Free: 87 of 100).

Lithuania: (Population: 2.8 M, rank 141, decrease 0.6%. Free: 91 of 100).

Estonia: (Population: 1.3 M, rank 155, decrease 0.2%. Free: 94 of 100).

Serbia: (including Kosovo: Population: 8.7 M, rank 97, decrease 0.3%. Free: 76 of 100).

Kosovo ((Disputed: recognized by 110 countries, and not recognized by Serbia, Russia, and others) Population: 1.8 M, Partly free: 52 of 100).

Turkey: (Population 80.7 M, rank 19, growth 1.2%. Partly free: 38 of 100).

Greece: (Population 11.1 M, rank 82, decrease 0.2%. Free: 84 of 100). 7 December 2018. Vladimir Putin held talks at the Kremlin with Greek Prime Minister Alexis Tsipras, who arrived in Russia on a working visit.

Republic of North Macedonia: (Population 2 M, rank 147, growth 0.1%. Partly Free: 57 of 100).

Albania: (Population 2.9 M, rank 139, growth 0.1%. Partly free: 68 of 100).

Cyprus: (Population 1.1 M, rank 159, growth 0.8%. Free: 94 of 100).

Kazakhstan (Population 18.2 M, rank 64, growth 1.2%. Not free: 22 of 100. Area 2.72 M km^2, rank 9.).

Armenia: (Population 2.9 M, rank 138, growth 0.2%. Partly free: 45 of 100).

Azerbaijan: (Population 9.8 M, rank 90, growth 1.1%. Not free 14 of 100).

Uzbekistan: (Population 31.9 M, rank 44, growth 1.5%. Not free: 3 of 100).

Kyrgyzstan (Population 6 M, rank 112, growth 1.5%. Partly free, 37 of 100).

Tajikistan: (Population 8.9 M, rank 96, growth 2.1%. Not free, 11 of 100).

Turkmenistan: (Population 5.7 M, rank 113, growth 1.7%. Not free, 4 of 100).

Washington (1790), Smithsonian National Museum of Natural History (1910, with wings added in the 1960s, with 126 millions of objects), on the National Mall, on Constitution Avenue NW.

United Kingdom, Canada, South America

United Kingdom: (Population: 66.1 M, rank 21, growth 0.6%. Free: 95 of 100).

Ireland: (Population: 4.7 M, rank 123, growth 0.8%. Free: 96 of 100)

Canada: (Population: 36.6 M, rank 38, growth 0.9%. Free: 99 of 100. Area 9.9 M km^2, rank 2). 13 December 2018. Reports: Canadian businessman Michael Spavor is being investigated on suspicion of harming China's state security, days after Chinese authorities detained former Canadian diplomat Michael Kovrig. The news follows the recent arrest of Huawei CFO Meng Wanzhou in Vancouver.

20 December 2018. Reports: China's foreign ministry said a Canadian woman is undergoing "administrative punishment" for working in the country illegally, marking the third Canadian to have been detained in China, following the arrest of Huawei CFO Meng Wanzhou in Vancouver.

Mexico: (Population: 129.1 M, rank 10, growth 1.3%. Partly Free: 65 of 100. Area 1.96 M km^2, rank 13). 3 December 2018. Reports: Andres Manuel Lopez Obrador has been sworn in as Mexico's next president, starting his six-year term with a promise to end corruption, poverty and extreme violence. The months since his election have been full of surprising news for observers. Most recently, he canceled a $13 B new Mexico City airport.

20 December 2018. Reports: As the battle continues over border wall funding and a government shutdown, the U.S. pledged $5.8 B in aid and investment for strengthening economic development in Central America, and another $4.8 B in development aid for southern Mexico. "I have a dream that I want to see become a reality... that nobody will want to go work in the United States anymore," newly inaugurated Mexican President Andres Manuel Lopez Obrador said before the announcement.

Chile: (Population: 18 M, rank 65, growth 0.8%. Free 94 of 100).

Colombia: (Population: 49 M, rank 29, growth 0.8%. Partly free 64 of 100).

Argentina: (Population: 44.2 M, rank 31, growth, 1%. Free: 82 of 100. Area 2.78 M km^2, rank 8.). 2 December 2018. Vladimir Putin held talks with President of the Argentine Republic, Mauricio Macri, at the Casa Rosada palace.

Brazil (Population: 209.2 M, rank 6, growth 0.8%. Free, 79 of 100. Area 8.5 M km^2, rank 5.). 2 January 2019. Reports: Jair Bolsonaro has been sworn in as Brazil's president, taking the reins of Latin America's largest and most populous nation. The former army captain told Congress he wanted a "national pact" to free Brazil of corruption, crime and economic mismanagement. He also promised to "create a new virtuous cycle to open markets", and "carry out important structural reforms", to shore up a growing public deficit.

Peru: (Population: 32.1 M, rank 5, growth 1.2%. Free: 72 of 100)

Cuba: (Population: 11.4 M, rank 42, growth 0.1%. Not free, 15 of 100). 1 January 2019. Xinhua. Chinese President Xi Jinping on Tuesday, 1 January 2019, warmly congratulated Raul Castro, first secretary of the Central Committee of the Communist Party of Cuba, and Miguel Diaz-Canel, president of the Council of State and the Council of Ministers of Cuba, on the 60th anniversary of Cuba's revolution victory on behalf of the Communist Party of China (CPC) and the Chinese government and people.

In his congratulatory message to Raul Castro, Xi, who is also general secretary of the CPC Central Committee, said under the strong leadership of the Communist Party of Cuba over the past 60 years, the Cuban government and people have made great achievements, with hard work, in the cause of socialist construction, which are highly appreciated and congratulated by the CPC and the Chinese government and people. The relations between the two parties and two countries have stood the test of international vicissitudes and achieved fruitful results, making the two sides good friends, good comrades and good brothers, Xi noted.

Xi said he attaches great importance to the development of the China-Cuba friendship and is willing to work together with Raul Castro to lead bilateral relations to keep marching forward.

In his congratulatory message to Diaz-Canel, Xi said that the Communist Party of Cuba and its people are endeavoring to update and improve the nation's socialist system, which will guarantee new developments in Cuba's socialist cause.

Xi mentioned Diaz-Canel's historic visit to China around a month ago, during which the two leaders proposed a blueprint for bilateral ties in the new era, adding that he is willing to join hands with Diaz-Canel for continuous development of China-Cuba relations.

Chinese Premier Li Keqiang also sent a congratulatory message to Diaz-Canel on Tuesday, saying Cuba has enjoyed flourishing national developments and will usher in a brighter future.

The two countries have always understood and supported each other, pushing bilateral relations for an all-round and in-depth development, said the premier.

Li also voiced hope that with the joint efforts from both sides, their traditional friendship will continue to bear fruits.

Bolivia: (Population: 11 M, rank 83, growth 1.5%. Partly free 68 of 100).

Paraguay: (Population: 6.8 M, rank 107, growth 1.3%. Partly free 64 of 100).

Panama: (Population: 4.1 M, rank 131, growth 1.6%. Free: 83 of 100).

Venezuela: (Population: 32 M, rank 43, growth 1.3%. Not free: 30 of 100). 5 December 2018. Vladimir Putin held talks with President of the Bolivarian Republic of Venezuela, Nicolas Maduro, at his Novo-Ogaryovo residence near Moscow, Russia.

Guyana: (Population 777K, (rank 165, grows 0.6%). Free: 74 of 100).

Trinidad and Tobago: (Population 1.3 M, (rank 153, grows 0.3%). Free: 81 of 100).

Nicaragua: (Population 6.2 M, (rank 110, grows 1.1%). Partly Free: 47 of 100).

New York (1624), 22 Nov 2007: on Broadway, close to Times Square, and to Times Square Tower (2004, 221 m, 47 floors).

France, Germany, and neighbors

France: (Population 64.9 M, rank 22, growth 0.4%. Free: 90 of 100). 3 December 2018. Reports: Emmanuel Macron is considering declaring a state of emergency, which allows authorities to prevent protests and other public gatherings. It follows the third weekend of violent demonstrations.

5 December 2018. Vladimir Putin met in Moscow, in a private meeting, with Francois Fillon, who was Prime Minister of the French Republic from 2007 to 2012.

7 December 2018. Reports: French President Emmanuel Macron will address France on the "yellow vest" movement early next week, as the country braces for another wave of violent weekend protests over the cost of living.

Reports: The "Yellow Vest" protests in France over the last month will cost the country's economy 0.1% in Q4, according to French Finance Minister Bruno Le Maire.

11 December 2018. Reports: Facing violent demonstrations over living costs, the French government is preparing for a Tuesday, 11 Dec, of protests by high-school students. Emmanuel Macron addressed the nation last night for the first time since the Gilet Jaunes demonstrations began, promising to raise the minimum wage and speed up tax relief. The concessions will likely cost the country between €8 B-€10 B.

28 December 2018. Reports: Russian aluminum giant Rusal has appointed independent non-executive director Jean-Pierre Thomas, from France, as its new chairman, as part of an agreed-upon restructuring. "Mr. Thomas has in-depth experience with Russian relations, having been tasked with several projects aimed at boosting economic cooperation between France and Russia," Rusal said in a disclosure.

Belgium (Population 11.4 M, rank 80, growth 0.6%. Free: 95 of 100). 19 December 2018. Reports: It's Europe's first government collapse over the U.N. migration deal signed in Marrakesh, Morocco, last week. Belgian Prime Minister Charles Michel has offered his resignation just days after losing the backing of the nationalist New Flemish Alliance, one of his main coalition partners. However, with only five months to go until planned legislative elections in May, it was not immediately clear whether King Philippe will accept Michel's departure.

European Commission, European Union, EU: 28 EU countries: Austria, Belgium, Bulgaria, Croatia, Republic of Cyprus, Czech Republic, Denmark, Estonia, Finland, France, Germany, Greece, Hungary, Ireland, Italy, Latvia, Lithuania, Luxembourg, Malta, Netherlands, Poland, Portugal, Romania, Slovakia, Slovenia, Spain, Sweden and the UK.

12 December 2018. Reports: The European Parliament is continuing its legislative sessions in Strasbourg, France, despite yesterday's terrorist attack in a local Christmas market that killed four people and injured eleven. A vote today is likely to approve an EU-Japan free trade pact. It will create the world's largest free trade area when it comes into force in early 2019.

Germany: (Population 82.1 M, rank 16, growth 0.2%. Free: 95 of 100). 7 December 2018. Reports: Germany's ruling Christian Democrats will vote to replace Angela Merkel as their leader today, with the successful candidate then a hot favorite to become future chancellor. Many delegates at the Hamburg congress say they will not make up their mind until they have heard the speeches of leading candidates, one who is seen as a choice for "more the same," and another one, Friedrich Merz, who appeals to the party's traditionally conservative supporters.

11 December 2018. Vladimir Putin had a telephone conversation with Chancellor of the Federal Republic of Germany, Angela Merkel, at the initiative of the German side.

The situation, resulting from the violation by Ukrainian vessels of the Russian Federation state border on November 25, was further discussed. The two leaders expressed mutual interest in preventing escalation in the waters of the Azov and Black seas, and in resolving the problems stemming from the provocative actions of the Ukrainian authorities.

Issues related to the Syrian crisis were touched upon, with emphasis on the priority of promoting the intra-Syrian dialogue, and the formation of the Constitutional Committee.

The two leaders also exchanged views on the situation in the area of strategic security, in light of the U.S. administration's intention to withdraw from the Intermediate-Range Nuclear Forces Treaty.

It was agreed to further maintain contact at various levels.

29 December 2018. Vladimir Putin had a telephone conversation with Federal Chancellor of the Federal Republic of Germany Angela Merkel. The two leaders extensively discussed the Syrian conflict, with a focus on the implementation of decisions reached by the four-party summit (Russia – Turkey – Germany – France), which took place on October 27 in Istanbul.

Vladimir Putin stressed that the work organized by the guarantor states of the Astana process, to compile a list of members of the Constitutional Committee, creates conditions for a long-term and stable settlement in Syria.

Vladimir Putin and Angela Merkel also discussed the plans of the United States to withdraw its troops from Syria.

Additionally, they exchanged opinions on developments following the Ukrainian provocation in the Kerch Strait on November 25.

Vladimir Putin and Angela Merkel wished each other a happy New Year and agreed to continue their contacts.

Norway (Population 5.3 M, rank 118, growth 1%. Free: 100 of 100).

Sweden (Population 9.9 M, rank 89, growth 0.7%. Free: 100 of 100). 3 December 2018. Reports: The world's first commercial license for an electric driverless truck is expected to be awarded by Sweden's Transport Agency in January 2019, according to the FT. Powered by the Nvidia Drive platform, Einride and DB Schenker's "smart container on wheels," called the T-Pod, is considered "Level 4" Autonomous. The vehicle also lacks a driver cabin, which can be half the cost of building a truck, offering more room for freight.

20 December 2018. Reports: Policymakers in Sweden have taken a decisive step away from an historic stimulus program, hiking interest rates for the first time in seven years. The krona soared on the news, appreciating as much as 1% against the euro, with the quarter of a percentage point increase bringing the repo rate to minus 0.25%. The need for a "highly expansionary monetary policy has

decreased slightly," according to the Riksbank, as inflation and inflation expectations are now looking "established."

The Netherlands (Population 17 M, rank 67, growth 0.3%. Free: 99 of 100).

Czech Republic (Population 10.6 M, rank 87, growth 0.1%. Free: 94 of 100).

Denmark (Population 5.7 M, rank 114, growth 0.4%. Free: 97 of 100. Area (including Greenland) 2.22 M km^2, rank 12 but not official).

Luxembourg (Population 583 K, rank 169, growth 1.3%. Free: 98 of 100).

Spain: (Population 46.3 M, rank 30, growth 0%. Free: 94 of 100). 20 December 2018. Reports: It's a big day for Spain's Socialist Prime Minister Pedro Sanchez, who will decree a 22% rise in the minimum wage that will take the country from being among the lowest base pay in Europe to one of the highest. The IMF and business groups say the move will lead to job losses.

Portugal: (Population 10.3 M, rank 88, decrease 0.4%. Free: 97 of 100). 3 December 2018. Lisbon, Portugal – TAP Air Portugal has taken delivery of the world's first new-generation widebody A330neo and, as the launch airline, will be the first to benefit from the aircraft's unbeatable operating economics, increased range, and Airbus' new Airspace cabin, offering passengers the best in class comfort. The Portuguese carrier will take delivery of a further 20 A330-900s in the coming years.

Liechtenstein: (Population: 38,000, rank 215, growth 0.7%, Free: 91 of 100)

India, Pakistan, Australia, and neighbors

India (Population: 1.3 B, rank 2nd, growth 1.1%. Free: 77 of 100. Area 3.28 M km^2, rank 7). 10 December 2018. Reports: Indian stocks are still holding on to gains for the year, but they're disappearing quickly. The BSE Sensex Index fell 2% today, marking its worst close in four weeks. Exit polls in regional elections showed Prime Minister Narendra Modi's party struggling in big heartland states, suggesting that farm distress, and a lack of jobs for younger people, could prove stumbling blocks for his re-election bid in May.

12 December 2018. Reports: Prime Minister Narendra Modi's government is likely to announce farm loan waivers worth as much as 4 T rupees ($56.5 B), government sources and analysts told Reuters. That would woo India's 263 M farmers ahead of a general election, after his ruling party suffered a rural defeat in state polls. The previous Congress party-led coalition government announced farm loan waivers in 2008, helping it return to power with a bigger mandate in 2009.

Indonesia: (Population: 263.9 M, rank 4, growth 1.1%. Partly free: 65 of 100. Area 1.91 M km^2, rank 14.). 23 December 2018. The President of Russia expressed condolences to President of Indonesia, Joko Widodo, over the tragic aftermath of the tsunami that hit coastal areas of the Sunda Strait, between Sumatra and Java Islands.

Australia: (Population: 24.4 M, rank 53, growth 1.3%. Free: 98 of 100. Area 7.69 M km^2, rank 6). Reports: Australia took the world's largest LNG exporter place from Qatar for the first time in November, according to data from Refinitiv Eikon. It follows the startup of a number of export projects in the country over the past three years, most recently the Ichthys project offshore its northern coast.

Reports: PERTH, Australia – Airbus Defense and Space announced the opening of the world's first High Altitude Pseudo-

Satellite (HAPS) flight base serving as the launch site for the Zephyr UAV in Wyndham, Western Australia. This site has been chosen due to its largely unrestricted airspace, and reliable weather, and is the result of significant investment by Airbus into its Zephyr program.

New Zealand: (Population 4.7 M, rank 125, growth 1%. Free: 98 of 100). 9 December 2018. Reports: The U.S. Congress is set to pass an inexcusable farm bill that increases subsidies, rather than reforming them. A conference committee is finalizing details on the budget buster bill, which will spend about $900 B over 10 years on farm subsidies and food stamps. These farm payments would come on top of the $12 B or so in subsidies the President is already handing out to farmers, to offset the damage of his trade war. Farm subsidies transfer income upwards, harm the economy, and are unfair to taxpayers footing the bill. They should be repealed. Like other businesses, farm businesses should provide their own safety nets by using market-based financial tools, and saving during the good years. U.S. agriculture would thrive without subsidies, as it has in subsidy-free New Zealand.

NASA sends CubeSats to space on first dedicated launch with partner Rocket Lab.

MAHIA PENINSULA, New Zealand - A series of new CubeSats now are in space, conducting a variety of scientific investigations and technology demonstrations, following launch Sunday, 16 Dec, of Rocket Lab's first mission for NASA, under a Venture Class Launch Services (VCLS) contract.

Pakistan: (Population 212 M, rank 5, growth 2%. Partly free: 43 of 100). 2 January 2019. Reports: China has pledged to lend at least $2 B to Pakistan to shore up its forex reserves, and prevent further devaluations of the rupee against the dollar, two senior government officials told the FT. The promised financial support comes as Islamabad negotiates a potential $7 B - $8 B loan with the IMF. The rupee has lost more than a fifth of its value against the dollar since late 2017, and Fitch last month cut Pakistan's debt rating deeper into junk territory.

Philippines: (Population 104.9 M, rank 13, growth 1.5%. Partly free 63 of 100).

Singapore: (Population 5.7 M, rank 115, growth 1.5%. Partly free 51 of 100).

31 December 2018. Reports: Already hit by low commodity prices and China's punitive trade tariffs, U.S. farmers are bracing for a tough 2019 as the refurbished Trans-Pacific Partnership came into effect. Known as CPTPP, the pact will slash tariffs among the 11 nations that cover 14% of global growth. It's already a reality for Australia, Canada, Japan, Mexico, New Zealand, Singapore and Vietnam, while the remaining four members - Brunei, Chile, Malaysia and Peru - are soon expected to follow suit.

The EAS currently comprises 18 countries: 10 ASEAN members (Brunei Darussalam, Cambodia, Indonesia, Laos, Malaysia, Myanmar, the Philippines, Singapore, Thailand and Vietnam), and eight dialogue partners: Russia (joined the EAS in 2010), the United States, Japan, South Korea, India, China, Australia and New Zealand.

APEC (21 members: Singapore, China, USA, Vietnam, Australia, Japan, Indonesia, Russia, Philippines, Malaysia, Hong Kong, Thailand, Chile, Canada, New Zealand, South Korea, Peru, Mexico, Brunei, Papua New Guinea, Chinese Taipei)

Thailand: (Population 69 M, rank 20, growth 0.3%. Not free 32 of 100).

Myanmar (Burma, Population 53.3 M, rank 26, growth 0.9%. Not free 32 of 100

Bangladesh (Population 164.6 M, rank 8, growth 1.1%. Partly free 47 of 100).

Sri Lanka (Population 20.8 M, rank 58, growth 0.4%. Partly free 56 of 100).

Malaysia (Population 31.6 M, rank 45, growth 1.34%. Partly free 44 of 100).

Brunei: (Population 428,000, rank 176, growth 1.3%. Not free 29 of 100).

Vanuatu: (Population 276,000, rank 185, growth 2.2%. Free 80 of 100)

Tonga: (Population 108,000, rank 195, growth 0.8%. Free 74 of 100

Papua New Guinea: (Population 8.2 M, rank 101, growth 2.1%, Partly Free 64 of 100). APEC (21 members: Singapore, China, USA, Vietnam, Australia, Japan, Indonesia, Russia, Philippines, Malaysia, Hong Kong, Thailand, Chile, Canada, New Zealand, South Korea, Peru, Mexico, Brunei, Papua New Guinea, Chinese Taipei)

Finland, Helsinki: the Railway Square, east of the railway station, with the Finnish National Theatre (1872 - 1902, left).

Italy, Middle East, Africa

Italy: (Population 59.3 M, rank 23, decrease 0.1%. Free: 89 of 100). 4 December 2018. Reports: Italian Prime Minister Giuseppe Conte said he will present a new budget proposal in the next few hours. The government intends to drop the proposed deficit to 2% for 2019, from a previous 2.4%, according to sources.

Beautiful houses in Murano, near Venezia, Italia.

12 December 2018. Reports: France risks EU censure over its latest "Gilets Jaunes" budget concessions, Italian Deputy Prime Minster Luigi Di Maio declared, adding that he expected Brussels to treat Paris and Rome in the same fashion. The European Commission has rejected Italy's draft budget which targets the deficit to rise to 2.4% of GDP in 2019, while France's 2019 deficit is now likely to rise above 3%. More news headlines are anticipated as Italy's Giuseppe Conte meets with Jean-Claude Juncker.

13 December 2018. Reports: Italian Prime Minister Giuseppe Conte is targeting a smaller budget deficit for next year, totaling 2.04% of GDP, down from 2.4%, the level his government

had previously earmarked to finance expansionary and costly measures. Italy's new plan is unlikely to satisfy the European Commission, but it will allow for more talks to proceed, and postpone any decision about disciplinary proceedings.

20 December 2018. Reports: Diego Piacentini, one of the most senior executives at Amazon who had previously led its international business, has left the company, after going on a two-year leave to work with the Italian government.

Vatican: (Population 792, rank 233 (last), decrease 1.1%).

San Marino: (Population 33,400, rank 218, growth 0.6%. Free 97 of 100)

Jordan (Population 9.7 M, rank 92, growth 2.6%. Partly free, 37 of 100).

Lebanon: (Population: 6 M, rank 111, growth 1.3%. Partly free: 44 of 100).

United Arab Emirates (UAE) (Population: 9.4 M, rank 94, growth 1.4%. Not free, 20 of 100).

Saudi Arabia (Population 32.9 M, rank 41, growth 2.1%. Not free: 10 of 100. Area 2.149 M km^2, rank 12.).

Yemen (Population 28.2 M, rank 50, growth 2.4%. Not free: 14 of 100).

Iraq (Population 38.2 M, rank 36, growth 2.9%. Not free: 27 of 100).

Iran: (Population 81.1 M, rank 18, growth 1.1%. Not free: 17 of 100. 26 December 2018. Reports: Iranian President Hassan Rouhani has announced a 20% increase in public sector wages, presenting a $42.7 B budget to parliament for next year.

Israel: (Population 8.3 M, rank 100, growth 1.6%. Free: 80 of 100). 8 December 2018. Vladimir Putin had a telephone conversation with Israeli Prime Minister, Benjamin Netanyahu, at the latter's initiative. Mr. Netanyahu informed the Russian leader on the details of the operation conducted by the Israeli armed forces along the demarcation line between Israel and Lebanon.

The President of Russia stressed the importance of ensuring stability in the region, in strict accordance with Resolution 1701 of the UN Security Council, with the UN Interim Force in Lebanon providing coordination. Speaking about Syria, Vladimir Putin underlined the need for better Russian-Israeli military cooperation.

In this context, the upcoming dialogue between the experts of the countries' defense ministries, as part of the joint working group, was referred to as a much-needed development.

The leaders agreed to consider holding another personal meeting.

Palestine: (Population 4.9 M (rank 121, grows 2.7%). Not free: 28 of 100).

Egypt (Population 97.5 M (rank 14, grows 1.9%). Not free, 26 of 100). 16 December 2018. Reports: In Egypt, in the Saqqara region, which is south of Cairo, a circa 4,460-year-old well-preserved tomb (10 m by 3 m by 3 m) was discovered, which is the final resting place of a royal priest called Wahtye, who served during Egypt's Fifth Dynasty (circa 2500 BC to 2350 BC, for 150 years) under the 3rd Pharaoh Neferirkare (Reign circa 2483 BC – 2465 BC, for 18 years). It contains two levels filled with dozens of statues and colorful drawings of the priest and his family, and it is in near-perfect condition. Its drawings are almost completely preserved, and the tomb itself had not been looted, according to Reuters.

League of Arab States (LAS) (22 countries: Algeria, Bahrein, Comoros, Djibouti, Egypt, Iraq, Jordan, Kuwait, Lebanon, Libya, Mauritania, Morocco, Oman, Palestine, Qatar, Saudi Arabia, Somalia, Sudan, Syria, Tunisia, United Arab Emirates and Yemen).

Qatar: (Population 2.6 M (rank 142, grows 2.7%). Not free: 26 of 100). 3 December 2018. Reports: Just days before a crucial OPEC meeting, Qatar announced plans to pull out of the oil cartel in January 2019.

Kuwait: (Population 4.1 M (rank 130, grows 2.1%). Partly free: 36 of 100).

Oman: (Population 4.6 M (rank 127, grows 4.8%). Not free: 25 of 100)

Bahrain: (Population 1.5 M (rank 152, grows 4.7%). Not free: 12 of 100).

Syria: (Population 18.2 M (rank 63, decrease 0.9%). Not free: 0 of 100).

Kenya: (Population 49.7 M (rank 28, growth 2.6%. Partly free, 51 of 100).

Libya: (Population 6.3 M, rank 109, growth 1.3%. Not free: 13 of 100). 7 December 2018. Reports: OPEC has kicked off another day of talks on oil production curbs, after a summit on Thursday, 6 Dec, ended with no deal, as Russia resisted the 1M bpd cut that Saudi Arabia was demanding. Other points: Iran sees no possibility of curbing its output. OPEC ministers are also discussing exemptions for Libya, Venezuela and Nigeria, which are opposed to participating in a supply reduction.

Algeria: (Area 2.38 M km^2, rank 10.)

Tunisia: (Population 11.5 M, rank 78, growth 1.1%. Free: 78 of 100).

Morocco: (Population 35.7 M, rank 39, growth 1.3%. Partly free: 41 of 100).

South Africa: (Population 56.7 M, rank 25, growth 1.3%. Free, 78 of 100).

Zimbabwe: (Population 16.5 M, rank 70, growth 2.4%. Partly Free, 32 of 100).

Sudan (Population 40.5 M, rank 35, growth 2.4%. Not Free: 6 of 100).

South Sudan (Population 12.5 M, rank 76, growth 2.8%. Not Free: 4 of 100)

Guinea: (Population 12.7 M, rank 75, growth 2.6%. Partly Free, 41 of 100).

Djibouti (Population 957,000, rank 160, growth 1.6%. Not Free: 26 of 100).

Somalia: (Population 14.7 M, rank 74, growth 3%. Not free: 5 of 100).

Niger (Population 21.4 M, rank 57, growth 3.9%. Partly free: 49 of 100).

Nigeria (Population 190.8 M, rank 7, growth 2.6%. Partly free: 50 of 100).

Cameroon (Population 24 M, rank 55, growth 2.6%. Not free: 24 of 100).

Sierra Leone: (Population 7.5 M (rank 103, grows 2.2%). Partly free: 66 of 100)

Chad: (Population 15 M (rank 73, grows 3.1%). Not free: 18 of 100).

The Gambia: (Population 2.1 M (rank 146, grows 3%). Not free: 20 of 100).

Malawi: (Population 18.6 M (rank 61, grows 2.9%). Partly free: 63 of 100).

Rwanda: (Population 12.2 M (rank 77, grows 2.4%). Not free: 24 of 100).

Burkina Faso: (Population 19.1 M (rank 60, grows 2.9%). Partly free: 63 of 100).

Central African Republic: (Population 4.6 M (rank 126, grows 1.4%). Not free: 10 of 100).

Senegal: (Population 15.8 M (rank 72, grows 2.8%). Free: 78 of 100).

Gabon: (Population 2 M (rank 149, grows 2.3%). Partly Free: 32 of 100).

Madagascar: (Population 25.5 M (rank 51, grows 2.7%). Partly Free: 56 of 100).

Democratic Republic of the Congo: (Population 81.3 M (rank 17, grows 3.3%). Not Free: 19 of 100. Area 2.34 M km^2, rank 11). Reports: The second-largest Ebola outbreak in history has spread to Butembo, a major city with more than 1 M residents in eastern Congo. Health experts now worry whether the stock of an experimental vaccine supplied by Merck will stand up to the epidemic's demands. According to Congo's health ministry, without the teams that have vaccinated more than 41 K people so far, the outbreak could have already seen more than 10 K Ebola cases (vs. the current 471).

Angola: (Population 29.7 M (rank 46, grows 3.4%). Not Free: 24 of 100).

Zambia: (Population 17 M (rank 66, grows 3%). Partly Free: 56 of 100).

United Republic of Tanzania: (Population 57 M (rank 24, grows 3.1%). Partly Free: 58 of 100).

Medical

Bacteria are present in nearly every breath we take. How the airway protects itself from infection caused by these bacteria has been largely unknown. A team of researchers at Mass. Eye and Ear discovered that when bacteria are inhaled, cells in the nose release tiny, fluid-filled sacs, called exosomes, that attack the bacteria. These exosomes also shuttle protective antimicrobial proteins from the front of the nose to the back, shielding other cells from the bacteria before it gets too far into the body. This finding, published online in the Journal of Allergy and Clinical Immunology (JACI), could pave the way for the development of new drug delivery techniques that harness this natural transport system – particularly for conditions in which medication is administered using nasal sprays, such as pain, nausea and seizures. This is the first study to demonstrate the immune system's innate ability to extend outside the body to maintain health. These findings may also help to explain how the body regulates "good" bacteria in the nose to maintain a healthy microbiome.

CLARITY enables the formation of a hydrogel matrix by crosslinking biological molecules to a 3D network of hydrophilic polymers followed by lipid removal to generate a transparent, structurally intact tissue. The tissue retains its original structural features, can be labeled with macromolecules, and subsequently imaged, without destruction of tissue morphology.

Researchers are working to expedite 3D analysis of normal and diseased tissues

Oregon State University engineers are using 3D animations techniques to increase the precision of radiation therapy for prostate cancer so that neighboring healthy tissues and organs are not affected. – Oregon State University, College of Engineering

Researchers present new virtual surgical simulator, known as "HandsOn.Surgery," at MEDICA 2018 in Germany.

The increased use of aggressive cleaners and disinfectants to prevent hospital-acquired infections (HAIs) has created an industry-wide problem of cracking in medical equipment housings. Proper material selection can prevent housing failures. When specialists evaluate chemical resistance for daily use in medical equipment housings, they must consider multiple factors, including the material's chemical compatibility under stress.

The developer of precision vascular robotics New Corindus announced its CorPath GRX System was successfully used in robotic-assisted coronary interventions.

Researchers at Moffitt Cancer Center are trying to devise alternative mechanisms to block KRas. Their recent study demonstrates that the protein GSK3 is an important mediator of KRas-dependent tumor viability.
Nature Communications, Dec-2018

University of Bristol Medical School researchers led a study that shows cemented metal-on-plastic hip replacements, less than 36 mm in diameter, are the most cost-effective in patients older than 65.

The tiny wearable device technology was designed by Northwestern Medicine along with Northwestern's McCormick School of Engineering scientists, and has the potential to monitor, separately and accurately, UVB and UVA exposure for people at high risk for melanoma.

A group at the University of Minnesota is using additive manufacturing for patient-specific organ models, sensors, and neural regeneration devices.

Alternate therapies for pain, the use of artificial intelligence in healthcare, and expanded window to treat stroke patients are some of the innovations that will enhance healing, and change healthcare in the coming year, according to a distinguished panel of doctors and researchers.

Older adults who take up drawing could enhance their memory, according to a new study. Researchers from the University of Waterloo found that even if people weren't good at it, drawing, as a method to help retain new information, was better than writing. – University of Waterloo, Experimental Aging and Research

A team from Brigham and Women's Hospital in Boston are developing a test that can detect tau protein, a calling card for Alzheimer's disease.

Not all memory loss is irreversible. Loss of memory can result from medication side effects, depression, certain medical conditions, and other controllable causes, which are reversible.

The robotic guidance and navigation system ExcelsiusGPS, which was launched in Europe, has already been used in surgeries in Germany, Italy, and Greece.

SUSU scientists developed a new rehabilitation device for people with leg injuries, which, unlike other analogous devices, allows involving all the joints of lower limb. Patented know-how can be applied for rehabilitation after serious injuries, and for other situations. – South Ural State University

Researchers at Johns Hopkins Medicine have identified in live human brains new radioactive "tracer" molecules that bind to and "light up" tau tangles, a protein associated with a number of neurodegenerative diseases including Alzheimer's disease. – Journal of Nuclear Medicine

Findings from a 2017 investigation published in the journal *Brain* support the idea that amyloid and tau must interact to cause Alzheimer's disease.

A surgical spray could prevent cancer from returning. Researchers have created a new spray gel, with immune-boosting drugs embedded inside, that could help prevent cancers from reoccurring after surgery.

When you're under stress, it can be even more difficult to maintain a healthy diet. Emotional eating can sabotage your attempt at achieving better health.

Loss of two genes drives a deadly form of colorectal cancer, but also reveals a potential treatment. Scientists from Sanford Burnham Prebys Medical Discovery Institute (SBP), in collaboration with clinicians from Scripps Clinic, have identified that the loss of two genes drives the formation of serrated colorectal cancer—yielding potential biomark for treatment. – Immunity

A molecular pathway, that's frequently mutated in many different forms of cancer, becomes active when cells push parts of their membranes outward into bulging protrusions, Johns Hopkins researchers report in a new study. The finding, published on Nov. 7, is pushing closer to a new cancer-fighting strategy. Johns Hopkins Medicine, Nature Communications

New research from Seattle Children's Research Institute and UW Medicine's Sports Health and Safety Institute found concussion rates among American football players ages 5-14 were higher than previously reported, with five out of every 100 youth, or 5%, suffering concussions. – Seattle Children's Hospital
The Journal of Pediatric

A new study in Ophthalmology Retina – a journal of the American Academy of Ophthalmology – shows that BB and pellet guns do blind children every year. And, the number of eye injuries related to such nonpowder guns are increasing at an alarming rate. – American Academy of Ophthalmology (AAO)
Ophthalmology Retina

Post-stroke depression stems from the cardiovascular changes in the brain that lead to a stroke in the first place. It's a type of depression that scientists are just now starting to probe, and want to use magnetic fields to treat it. – West Virginia University

Biomedical engineers at Georgia Tech developed a smartphone app that uses photos of a patient's fingernails, to determine whether the level of hemoglobin in their blood seems low.

The eyes may hold a surprising clue about the current state of stress – in an experiment, the more stressed people became, the smaller their pupils were.

First-ever digital 3D brain cell atlas was created by specialists.

Mariner Endosurgery has received a permission from FDA for an augmented surgical navigation system.

A tiny device at Nottingham University Hospital in Nottingham, England, is making it easier for pediatric transplant patients, and their caregivers, to collect blood samples at home for therapeutic drug monitoring.

An updated model of a cycle-tracking bracelet offers women new and customizable features. This fertility tracker guarantees pregnancy within one year.

Smell loss, or anosmia, affects approximately 5% of the general population. Some cases can be treated by caring for an underlying cause, such as a nasal obstruction. Others are much more complex, such as a head injury, or virus that damages the sensory nerves of the nose. For these cases, there are currently no effective therapies. Physicians at Massachusetts Eye and Ear recently found, for the first time, that placing electrodes in the nose induced sense of smell in humans by stimulating nerves in the olfactory bulb, a part of the brain that processes and relays smell information from the nose. Their findings, published online in the journal International Forum of Allergy & Rhinology, open the door to developing an implant technology that will restore sense of smell to those who have lost it.

Biosimilar to Genentech's Herceptin received FDA approval.

FDA approved Nplate for pediatric patients with immune thrombocytopenia.

Italia, Venezia, Procuratie Vecchie (circa 1520, left), Basilica di San Marco (828 – 1071, back), Campanile (1156, restored 1514, rebuilt 1912, right).

Researcher shows the two most common means of resistance to BRAF and MEK inhibitors are actually connected processes, with one activating the other, and can be targeted by other therapies.
– Perelman School of Medicine at the University of Pennsylvania Cancer Discovery

EC approved Merck's Keytruda as adjuvant therapy for resected stage III melanoma.

Study shows taltz superior to humira for patients with active psoriatic arthritis.

Male sex hormones (androgens), especially testosterone, are required to maintain the size and function of the prostate. As a result, a treatment option for intermediate-and high-risk prostate cancers is to interfere with the effects of androgens by blocking the testicles' production of testosterone or blocking the receptor to which testosterone attaches. Hormone therapy causes the cancer to regress, and is used routinely along with radiation therapy for the treatment of intermediate- and high-risk cancers, and in the management of metastatic prostate cancer.

When used for the treatment of metastatic prostate cancer, prostate cancer cells eventually bypass the testosterone block by manufacturing their own needed androgens through alternate pathways. Therefore, although hormone therapy is useful in treating prostate cancer, it does not offer a cure. Hormone therapy used to be reserved for men whose prostate cancer had spread to the lymph nodes, bone, or other sites. Now it is often given preemptively to men whose cancer is expected to spread after radiation or surgery—for example, a man with a rapidly rising PSA level.

For men with prostate cancer that has spread to lymph nodes or bones, the goals of hormone therapy are to prolong life and relieve symptoms such as bone pain or urinary tract problems. Hormone therapy prolongs life for many of these men; about 25 percent will live five or more years.

PSA level helps predict survival in men with metastatic prostate cancer. A PSA of less than 4 ng/mL within three to six months of initiating hormone therapy predicts a good response to the treatment. A rising PSA level during hormone therapy indicates that the disease is progressing. No consensus exists concerning when hormone therapy should begin. Whether hormone treatment is started before or after cancer progression is documented on a bone scan may or may not affect how long a man survives.

Moreover, all effective forms of hormone therapy have significant side effects. These side effects may include ED (which affects about 90 percent of men), loss of libido, breast enlargement, weight gain, loss of muscle mass, osteoporosis (decreased bone mass), fatigue, a decline in cognitive function, and hot flashes. Hormone therapy also increases the risk of cardiovascular disease in some men, and the harm may outweigh the benefit, especially for men with localized cancer who are unlikely to experience improved cancer control when hormone therapy is used in addition to other management options. Because no hormone treatment can cure the disease regardless of when treatment begins, side effects must be given serious consideration when deciding when to start the treatment.

There are many options for hormone therapy of prostate cancer. Surgical castration (surgical removal of the testes, which produce about 95 percent of a man's testosterone) was the main approach prior to the 1980s. Today the most common approach is the use of medications that interfere with the production of testosterone by the testes (medical castration) or block it from attaching to receptors inside cancer cells. These medications include luteinizing hormone-releasing hormone (LHRH) agonists, also known as gonadotropin-releasing hormone (GnRH) agonists; LHRH antagonists, also known as GnRH receptor antagonists; and antiandrogens. Whether accomplished surgically or medically, hormone therapy prolongs the life of men with metastatic prostate cancer.

Predict and prevent: the emergence of real-time sensor-based care. Wearables are being used for everything from smoking cessation to epilepsy management.

A study from researchers at Indiana University has found that CBD -- a major chemical component in marijuana -- appears to increase pressure inside the eye of mice, suggesting the use of the substance in the treatment of glaucoma may actually worsen it.

FDA approved lynparza for 1st-line maintenance therapy in advanced ovarian cancer.

Stem cell shots were linked to bacterial infection outbreak.

Latex hazard leads to recall of certain Dyural-40 and Dyural-80 Convenience Kit.

Bayer has already decided to stop selling the birth control device Essure, but FDA says it will continue to monitor the long-term safety of Essure.

Paragonix gets FDA approval for pediatric heart transport device. The Braintree, MA-based firm's Paragonix SherpaPak Cardiac Transport System also has clearance for the adult patient population.

Nowadays, encouraging people to eat a wide variety of foods may backfire and lead to consumption of more food, especially unhealthy items, and to weight gain, according to a recent advisory from the American Heart Association (AHA), published in *Circulation*. After reviewing research published since 2000, it concluded that there's no consistent evidence that greater overall dietary diversity promotes healthy weight or optimal eating.

Instead of recommending eating a variety of foods, the AHA concluded that dietary guidance should emphasize adequate consumption of fresh or minimally processed plant foods, such as vegetables, fruit, beans, and whole grains, as well as low-fat dairy products, nuts, poultry, and fish—along the lines of the DASH (Dietary Approaches to Stop Hypertension) diet and the AHA's own heart healthy dietary advice. There's no reason to increase variety if that means adding red meat, refined grains, sweets, sugary drinks, and all the other highly processed foods beckoning at markets.

Having too many choices at a meal can lead to overconsumption (the "smorgasbord effect"), in part, because eating foods with different flavors and sensory qualities may delay the feeling of satiety, and actually whet the appetite, even when people feel full—which is why there always seems to be "room for dessert." It's also easier to overfill your plate when you have a large number of choices. In contrast, you're likely to eat less if you have less variety, since foods similar in taste and texture dull the palate.

Therefore, it is recommended to stick to your shopping list at the market, and skip the aisles filled with junk food. Be especially careful at all-you-can-eat buffets and parties, where food is abundant. At home, serve a limited—but balanced—selection of healthful foods at meals. Using smaller plates also helps limit your choices, and the total amount of food you serve yourself.

There is growing criticism of video games for being violent, leading to myopia and addiction among young users.

If the knees make unusual noises when moving, those pops and clicks one hears coming from the knees may be the sound of arthritis beginning to take hold.

Researchers have made significant advances in diagnosing and treating diabetic retinopathy, one of the most serious complications of diabetes. Even so, diabetic retinopathy remains a leading cause of new cases of blindness among adults in the developed world. Fortunately, there is plenty that individuals with diabetes can do to protect their vision, even if they already have early signs of diabetic retinopathy.

Effective management of diabetes in the early stages is the best way to prevent or minimize future complications. People with prediabetes can prevent their condition from worsening, while those who have been diagnosed with diabetes have effective ways to monitor their condition and control their blood glucose levels.

People who have a stroke are about twice as likely to develop dementia, as people who don't have a stroke, according to a review of studies involving 3.2 millions of people—mostly older adults—worldwide. The analysis, conducted by the University of Exeter Medical School in England, and the University of Michigan, didn't report whether risk of dementia was higher for ischemic strokes (the most common kind, caused by a blood clot), or hemorrhagic strokes (caused by an artery bleeding in the brain). The findings were published online in August in *Alzheimer's & Dementia*. You can help prevent a stroke by getting high blood pressure and diabetes under control, engaging in regular physical activity, consuming heart-healthy foods, maintaining a healthy weight, and not smoking.

DNA sequencing can be used to identify the underlying genetic cause of many rare types of chronic kidney disease, leading to better treatment, finds a new study from Columbia University. Therefore, for patients with kidney disease, genetic testing may soon be routine. New England Journal of Medicine, December 26, 2018

Some dermal fibroblasts can convert into fat cells that reside under the dermis, giving skin a youthful look, and producing peptides that fight infections. UC San Diego researchers identified how skin ages, and loses fat and immunity, because of these dermal fibroblasts, which stop converting. University of California San Diego Health, Immunity

Getting plenty of exercise can help people live longer, but even brief bouts of huffing and puffing confer important health benefits. This guidance is from the most recent Physical Activity Guidelines for Americans issued by the U.S. Department of Health and Human Services. These science-based guidelines, which were published November 20, 2018, in *JAMA*, were written by a committee of health experts, and update recommendations issued in 2008. The new recommendations stress that any increase in physical activity fights disease, especially if you are currently sedentary. Here are the basics: Adults should engage in some form of moderately intense exercise, such as brisk walking, for at least 150 minutes a week, though more minutes means more benefit.
If you prefer vigorous exercise, such as jogging, 75 to 150 minutes is a good goal. Work your muscles with weights, elastic bands, or other forms of resistance training at least twice a week. Older men and women should also do balance exercises, such as walking backward or doing lunges (which you can look up online).
Earlier guidelines suggested that only bouts of physical activity of 10 minutes or more counted toward your weekly total, but the new recommendations state that every little bit helps. Simply sitting less and moving more can help lead you to better health.

A new study suggests that people over age 65, who are newly diagnosed with heart failure, can continue to drink moderate amounts of alcohol without worsening their condition.

New research regarding prostate cancer recommends two or more servings a week of fatty fish such as salmon, and no omega-3 capsules.

Mathematics, Science & Artificial Intelligence (AI)

Alternative energy sources are a way to rational resource saving. Development of nanotechnology is a serious impulse for development of alternative energy sources. For several years, scientists of South Ural State University have been working on creation of materials for a new generation of solar batteries.

A successful rocket launch on Monday, 3 Dec, by SpaceX marked twin milestones for the company's drive to ease access for commercial satellites into orbit. The mission was SpaceX's 19th launch this year, topping its previous record of 18 in 2017 The Falcon 9 rocket also carried the largest number of satellites - a cluster of more than five dozen - ever stacked on top a U.S. booster.

The automation revolution continues as robot janitors come to Walmart. Hundreds of the Zamboni-style floor scrubbers, made by San Diego-based startup Brain Corp., will begin cleaning in stores - even when customers are around - by the end of January 2019. Walmart has already been experimenting with automation, such as the scanning of shelves for out-of-stock items, and hauling products from storage for online orders.

A team of materials scientists from Penn State, Cornell and Argonne National Laboratory have, for the first time, visualized the 3D atomic and electron density structure of the most complex perovskite crystal structure system decoded to date. – Penn State Materials Research Institute, Nature Communications Dec-2018

AI could become the new quality control element in medical device manufacturing. By applying predictive analytics, medical device companies can make a shift to a proactive mode, to avoid potential problems before they happen, according to an expert in business strategy and software engineering.

In the Russian Federation, the paved road network is growing 7 times less per million people than in the developed countries of Europe and in the U.S.A. Because of the large and frequent defects of the road surface, the average speed of auto transport is lower than in Europe and the U.S.A. South Ural State University is working on a new concrete paving machine to improve the quality of roads.

An experiment has demonstrated, for the first time, electronic switching in an unusual, ultrathin material that can carry a charge with nearly zero loss at room temperature. Researchers hope to find. a new kind of transistor. – Lawrence Berkeley National Laboratory, Nature, Dec. 10, 2018

The partnership between Edwards Lifesciences and Bay Labs continues the trend of larger medtech firms teaming up with companies in the artificial intelligence space, to enhance existing medical devices.

Artificial intelligence and machine learning are forecast to be decisive technology changers for manufacturers and distributors through the next decade.

Google launched an AI program for eye disease.

Researchers are working on new ideas for colorants, or colorant additive packages, to provide polyesters (Polybutylene terephthalate [PBT]) formulations with bright orange colors, and in which the color is kept during the final product application, and the additive is thermally stable during processing of the formulation and application of the final product.

Grains in storage facilities, or in transit, are often protected with pesticides. Specialists are working to discover new approaches for long-term grain protection, without the reliance on chemical pesticides.

Engineers are seeking a high-performance technology for the disinfection of cooling water in existing evaporative towers, adopting new approaches, and overcoming the conventional processes.

Specialists are working on the best available methods to recycle and reuse the materials in the wind turbine blades, in order to be more sustainable, under a circular economy perspective.

U.S. solar installations in Q3 fell 30%, to 678 megawatts, from a year ago, as the administration's tariffs on overseas-made panels forced developers to put off large projects.

A Virgin Galactic rocket plane reached space and returned safely on Thursday, 13 Dec, becoming the first U.S. commercial human flight to exit Earth's atmosphere since the U.S. shuttle program ended in 2011.
Virgin Galactic was successful in sending humans to FAA definition of space for the first time
MOJAVE, Calif., - On Thursday, 13 Dec, Virgin Galactic successfully sent its SpaceShip Two "VSS Unity" 51.4 miles (82.7 km) above the surface of Earth. The pilots of the craft were Mark "Forger" Stucky and Frederick "CJ" Sturckow, who will be formally recognized by the FAA early next year with FAA Commercial Astronaut Wings. Sturckow will become the first person awarded NASA and FAA wings. He piloted NASA space shuttles four times.

An ongoing partnership between Wichita State University and Westar Energy recently resulted in the implementation of a new technology aimed at protecting wind turbine blades from lightning strikes.

Rocket Lab launched its third Electron rocket this year, early Sunday, 16 Dec, morning, in the company's first mission for NASA, that sent 13 spacecraft to orbit. The firm is the first to fly under NASA's Venture Class Launch Services program, which the U.S. government hopes to push the boundaries of cheap, reliable launches with the promising market of new small rocket services.

The lack of knowledge of the soil contribution to damping in offshore foundations for wind turbines has an impact on energy costs for utility-scale offshore wind installations, since this unknown requires designers to oversize structures, hence making them costlier.

Inflatable Stand-Up Paddles (SUP) have provided great flexibility to enthusiasts, and allowed the sport to grow in popularity. However, manually or electrically pumping the SUPs to the needed pressure is still cumbersome and time-consuming. Hence, the specialists are looking for a new user-friendly inflation system that can quickly inflate a 300L SUP and reach 20 PSI.

Because of the need to increase the trust in autonomous response in high consequence situations, researchers are looking for a method with the ability to assess the relative meaning and importance of new or changing information, and convey or explain the basis of recommendations in human terms, such that individuals can comprehend and manage on their own.

Marking its first national security space mission for the U.S. military, a SpaceX rocket carrying a $500 M GPS satellite built by Lockheed Martin blasted off from Florida's Cape Canaveral on Sunday, 23 Dec. The successful Falcon 9 launch is a significant victory for the privately held space company, which has spent years trying to break into the military space launch market dominated by United Launch Alliance, a partnership between Boeing and Lockheed.

Reports: The number of space launches from China this year was 37, making China the top in the world for space launches for the first time. This follows a launch on Tuesday, December 25, 2018 of a telecommunication satellite. The 31st and final space launch of 2018 in the United States took place on December 23, with the US Air Force contracting SpaceX to put up the first satellite for an updated GPS system. Third place Russia with 16, fourth the European Space Agency with 11, fifth India with 7, and sixth Japan had 6 launches this year. Total 108 launches.

Taking part in the worldwide search for fuel cell cathode materials, researchers at the University of Akron developed a new method of synthesizing catalysts from a combination of metals—platinum and nickel. They illuminate nanoparticle growth with x-rays. Brookhaven National Laboratory, Nature Communications

USA, Boston (founded in 1630): on a visiting tall ship, at the Boston Fish Pier (opened in 1915).

General news and issues

Amazon is testing its cashier-less checkout technology for bigger stores, sources tell the WSJ.

Mojave, Calif., – Virgin Orbit reported a successful test flight earlier this month of its modified Boeing 747-400 that was carrying a 21.3 m air-launched satellite delivery rocket under its port wing, where a fifth engine can be mounted on the aircraft.

Cybercriminals' computer virus WannaCry crippled more than 200,000 computers running Microsoft Windows in 150 countries in May 2017, bringing to a halt business for organizations around the globe, like Britain's National Health Service, Germany's Deutsche Bahn, Denmark's Maersk and FedEx in the United States. And while the aerospace industry was largely spared in the initial attack, in March of this year, Boeing was attacked by cybercriminals' WannaCry at its plant in Charleston, SC.
People ask the authorities to arrest the cybercriminals.

Amazon is looking at bringing its futuristic checkout-free store format to airports, according to public records and Reuters sources. Seven Amazon Go stores have already been opened to the public since January: in Chicago, San Francisco and Seattle. More than 350 M passengers boarded flights at the country's top 12 airports last year, according to the U.S. Department of Transportation.

It is well known that change, risk and hard work are things most people want nothing to do with.

Reports: A Texas elementary school speech pathologist refused to sign a pro-Israel oath, now mandatory in many states — so she lost her job.

One of the world's most famous Christmas carols, "Silent Night," marks its 200th anniversary on Christmas Eve, 2018.

The ammonia oxidizing archaea, or Thaumarchaeota, are amongst the most abundant marine microorganisms. Yet, we are still discovering which factors allow them to thrive in the ocean: A new publication reveals that marine Thaumarchaeota have a broader versatility than others. – University of Vienna, Nature Microbiology

In an update on its first employee buyout offer in 13 years, Verizon said about 10,400 have been accepted as part of the voluntary separation offer. It comes as the largest U.S. wireless carrier, by subscribers, works to cut $10 B in costs and upgrade to a faster 5G network. At the end of the third quarter, Verizon had 152,300 employees on its payroll.

Reports: Walmart is insisting on automation, and is in the early stages of testing a kitchen robot assistant, named "Flippy", at its headquarters in Bentonville, Arkansas. While Flippy can grill up to 150 burgers an hour, Walmart is interested in using the robot to fry foods - up to eight baskets at a time - for its in-stores delis. The machine costs between $60 K and $100 K depending on its features.

"All human beings are born free and equal in dignity and rights." This is the first sentence of the Universal Declaration of Human Rights. On 10 December 1948, 56 member states of the United Nations agreed on a catalogue of inalienable rights valid for all people.

Reports: Amazon is taking its cashier-free shops in a new, smaller direction. Located in one of the company's Seattle offices, the eighth Amazon Go store is about a quarter of the size of its predecessors, at a mere 450 square feet. Such small stores could help Amazon broaden its bricks-and-mortar footprint, and keep ahead of startups, which are trying to convince existing retailers to buy their cashier-less technology.

Verizon will book a $4.6 B accounting charge related to its Oath media business, after creating the unit by spending $9 B on acquiring AOL in 2015, and then Yahoo in 2017. Verizon hoped the combination would make it a more powerful force in digital advertising, but its share of that market has shrunk instead. Unable to turn the tide, the company recently scaled back its internet ambitions.

534 B.C. is the year when the theatre was born in Athens. A priest of Dionysus (a god of fertility and wine in Greece), by the name of Thespis, engages in a dialogue with the chorus, becoming the first actor. Thespis is also the first winner of a theatrical award. He takes the prize in the first competition for tragedy, held in Athens in 534 BC.

Amazon's influence and impact on B2C will transform B2B from a standard e-commerce storefront, to a highly personalized "modern commerce" approach, that provides customers with immediate transparent pricing, based on comprehensive data analysis.

Reports: One reason so many hundreds of important people are persuaded that the sky is falling is that they are paid handsomely to do so. In America and around the globe governments have created a multi-billion-dollar Climate Change Industrial Complex. A lot of people are getting really rich off of the climate change industry. According to a recent report by the U.S. Government Accountability Office, Federal funding for climate change research, technology, international assistance, and adaptation has increased from $2.4 B in 1993 to $11.6 B in 2014, with an additional $26.1 B for climate change programs and activities provided by the American Recovery and Reinvestment Act in 2009.

Reports: "The data clearly indicate that being able to read is not a requirement for graduation at (Madison) East, especially if you are black or Hispanic".

Reports: Debt worldwide hits record $184 Trillions.

"Amazon customers made this holiday season record-breaking with more items ordered worldwide than ever before," according to a company press release. Consumers purchased millions more Amazon Devices, and tens of millions of people worldwide started Prime free trials, or began paid memberships.

More than 50% of items sold in Amazon's stores this holiday season also came from small and medium-sized businesses.

There are movies, as well as real stories of megalomaniacs who become embittered, delusional, and alone, when their hubris (in Greek tragedy, like Achilles - excessive pride, especially pride and ambition so great that they offend the gods, and lead to one's downfall) alienates friends and enemies alike.

Reports: Amazon is planning to build and expand Whole Foods stores across the U.S., to put more customers within range of its two-hour delivery service called Prime Now, WSJ reports. The push, which would likely focus on regions in Western North America, is a shift from the layoffs and slowing store growth Whole Foods experienced for several years before Amazon bought it for $13.5 B in 2017.

Reports: More than three dozen drugmakers began 2019 by raising the cost of hundreds of medicines, according to an analysis from Rx Savings Solutions. The average increase was 6.3%, including rises on different doses for the same drug, as pressure grows on the industry over prices. Other companies, like Allergan, set the pace with increases of nearly 10% on more than two dozen products.

Humor

An old professor of liberal arts complains to a younger one of engineering:
- Let me tell you something: the liberal arts were murdered!
- No, responds the engineering professor, they committed suicide.

Finland, Helsinki Central railway station (1907 – 1914), on Brunnsgatan, in the city center.

Universe Axioms

Formulated by Michael M. Dediu

The following axioms are not independent of each other. They express in different ways the same concept of infinity.

Axiom 1. Pointing a theoretical laser from Earth, in any direction, at any time, after a finite amount of time the laser beam will touch an astronomic body.

Axiom 2. In any direction in space starting from Earth, at any time, there is an astronomic body from which the Earth can be theoretically seen.

Axiom 3. Infinity of space: Any straight line passing through the Earth's center intersects an infinite number of astronomic bodies.

Axiom 4. Infinity of time: Representing the time on a line, with the origin at the beginning of the year 1, the time goes to infinite in both positive and negative directions.

Axiom 5. Infinity of life: Because of the infinity of space and time, it is normal to consider that the life exists at any time, in an infinite number of places. Therefore right now, when you are reading this book, there is life outside the Earth, in an infinite number of places, but we do not know yet how to contact them.

Axiom 6. The Earth rotates itself around its polar axis, the Moon and many artificial satellites rotate around the Earth, in the Solar System all the planets and many other objects rotate around the Sun, the Solar System itself rotates around the center of the Milky Way galaxy, the Milky Way galaxy and all the billions of galaxies in our Universe (denoted U_1) rotate around the center of our Universe U_1, our Universe U_1, together with billions of other similar Universes, are inside a bigger Universe U_2 and rotate around the center of U_2, then U_2 and many others like it are inside a bigger U_3 and rotate around the center of U_3, and so on. Therefore, in general, the Universe U_n together with many similar Universes are inside the bigger Universe U_{n+1} and rotate around the center of U_{n+1}, for any n natural number, which goes to infinity. This can be written in the formula:

$$U_1 \subset U_2 \subset U_3 \subset \ldots \subset U_n \subset U_{n+1} \subset \ldots, \text{ n natural number.}$$

UK, Oxford, Oriel College (1326, in the east range of First quadrangle, the ornate portico in the center, with the inscription Regnante Carolo).

Time Axioms

Formulated by Michael M. Dediu

Axiom 1. Time is the most important force in the Univers.

Axiom 2. Everything is a function of time.

Axiom 3. Time exists in absolutely everything.

Axiom 4. Time creates and distroys everything.

Axiom 5. Time is invisible, inodor, insipid, unpalpabil, unaudible, but exists evrywhere.

Axiom 6. There are infinitezimal time particles, without mass, which are present everywhere, and which actually continuously transform everything.

UK, Cambridge, From Trinity Lane looking south to the west part of the northern façade and entrance of King's College Chapel (1446).

Bibliography

"The Histories" by Polybius
"Discours de la Méthode" by René Descartes
"Meditationes de prima philosophia" by René Descartes
"Philosophiae Naturalis Principia Mathematica" by Isaac Newton
Chinese encyclopedia Gujin Tushu Jicheng (Imperial Encyclopedia)
"Encyclopédie" by Jean-Baptiste le Rond d'Alembert and Denis Diderot
"Encyclopaedia Britannica" by over 4,400 contributors
"Encyclopedia Americana" by Francis Lieber

Michael M. Dediu is also the author of these books (which can be found on Amazon.com, and www.derc.com):

1. Aphorisms and quotations – with examples and explanations
2. Axioms, aphorisms and quotations – with examples and explanations
3. 100 Great Personalities and their Quotations
4. Professor Petre P. Teodorescu – A Great Mathematician and Engineer
5. Professor Ioan Goia – A Dedicated Engineering Professor
6. Venice (Venezia) – a new perspective. A short presentation with photographs
7. La Serenissima (Venice) - a new photographic perspective. A short presentation with many photos
8. Grand Canal – Venice. A new photographic viewpoint. A short presentation with many photos
9. Piazza San Marco – Venice. A different photographic view. A short presentation with many photos
10. Roma (Rome) - La Città Eterna. A new photographic view. A short presentation with many photos
11. Why is Rome so Fascinating? A short presentation with many photos
12. Rome, Boston and Helsinki. A short photographic presentation
13. Rome and Tokyo – two captivating cities. A short photographic presentation
14. Beautiful Places on Earth – A new photographic presentation

15. From Niagara Falls to Mount Fuji via Rome - A novel photographic presentation

16. From the USA and Canada to Italy and Japan - A fresh photographic presentation

17. Paris – Why So Many Call This City Mon Amour - A lovely photographic presentation

18. The City of Light – Paris (La Ville-Lumière) - A kaleidoscopic photographic presentation

19. Paris (Lutetia Parisiorum) – the romance capital of the world - A kaleidoscopic photographic view

20. Paris and Tokyo – a joyful photographic presentation. With a preamble about the Universe

21. From USA to Japan via Canada – A cheerful photographic documentary

22. 200 Wonderful Places, In The Last 50 Years – A personal photographic documentary

23. Must see places in USA and Japan - A kaleidoscopic photographic documentary

24. Grandeurs of the World - A kaleidoscopic photographic documentary

25. Corneliu Leu – writer on the same wavelength as Mark Twain. An American viewpoint

26. From Berkeley to Pompeii via Rome – A kaleidoscopic photographic documentary

27. From America to Europe via Japan - A kaleidoscopic photographic documentary

28. Discover America and Japan - A photographic documentary

29. J. R. Lucas – philosopher on a creative parallel with Plato, An American viewpoint

30. From America to Switzerland via France - A photographic documentary

31. From Bretton Woods to New York via Cape Cod - A photographic documentary

32. Splendid Places on the Atlantic Coast of the U. S. A. - A photographic documentary

33. Fourteen nice Cities on three Continents - A photographic documentary

34. 17 Picturesque Cities on the World Map - A photographic documentary

35. Unforgettable Places from Four Continents, including Trump buildings - A photographic documentary

36. Dediu Newsletter, Volume 1, Number 1, 6 December 2016 – Monthly news, review, comments and suggestions for a better and wiser world

37. Dediu Newsletter, Volume 1, Number 2, 6 January 2017 (available also at www.derc.com).

38. Dediu Newsletter, Volume 1, Number 3, 6 February 2017 (available at www.derc.com).

39. London and Greenwich, - A photographic documentary

40. Dediu Newsletter, Volume 1, Number 4, 6 March 2017 (available also at www.derc.com).

41. Dediu Newsletter, Volume 1, Number 5, 6 April 2017 (available also at www.derc.com).

42. Dediu Newsletter, Volume 1, Number 6, 6 May 2017 (available also at www.derc.com).

43. Dediu Newsletter, Volume 1, Number 7, 6 June 2017 (available also at www.derc.com).

44. London, Oxford and Cambridge, A photographic documentary

45. Dediu Newsletter, Volume 1, Number 8, 6 July 2017 (available also at www.derc.com).

46. Dediu Newsletter, Volume 1, Number 9, 6 August 2017 (available also at www.derc.com).

47. Dediu Newsletter, Volume 1, Number 10, 6 September 2017 (available also at www.derc.com).

48. Three Great Professors: President Woodrow Wilson, Historian German Arciniegas, and Mathematician Gheorghe Vranceanu – A chronological and photographic documentary

49. Dediu Newsletter, Volume 1, Number 11, 6 October 2017 (available also at www.derc.com).

50. Dediu Newsletter, Volume 1, Number 12, 6 November 2017 (available also at www.derc.com).

51. Dediu Newsletter, Volume 2, Number 1 (13), 6 December 2017 (available also at www.derc.com).

52. Two Great Leaders: Augustus and George Washington - A chronological and photographic documentary

53. Dediu Newsletter, Volume 2, Number 2 (14), 6 January 2018 (available also at www.derc.com).

54. Newton, Benjamin Franklin, and Gauss, A chronological and photographic documentary

55. Dediu Newsletter, Volume 2, Number 3 (15), 6 February 2018 (available also at www.derc.com).

56. 2017: World Top Events, But Many Little Known, A chronological and photographic documentary

57. Dediu Newsletter, Volume 2, Number 4 (16), 6 March 2018 (available also at www.derc.com).

58. Vergilius, Horatius, Ovidius, and Shakespeare - A chronological and photographic documentary.

59. Dediu Newsletter, Volume 2, Number 5 (17), 6 April 2018 (available also at www.derc.com).

60. Dediu Newsletter, Volume 2, Number 6 (18), 6 May 2018 (available also at www.derc.com).

61. Vivaldi, Bach, Mozart, and Verdi - A chronological and photographic documentary.

62. Dediu Newsletter, Volume 2, Number 7 (19), 6 June 2018 (available also at www.derc.com).

63. Dediu Newsletter, Volume 2, Number 8 (20), 6 July 2018 (available also at www.derc.com).

64. Dediu Newsletter, Volume 2, Number 9 (21), 6 August 2018 (available also at www.derc.com).

65. World History, a new perspective - A chronological and photographic documentary.

66. World Humor History with over 100 Jokes, a new perspective - A chronological and photographic documentary

67. Dediu Newsletter, Volume 2, Number 10 (22), 6 September 2018 (available also at www.derc.com).

68. Dediu Newsletter, Volume 2, Number 11 (23), 6 October 2018 (available also at www.derc.com).

69. Dediu Newsletter, Volume 2, Number 12 (24), 6 November 2018

70. Da Vinci, Michelangelo, Rembrandt, Rodin - A chronological and photographic documentary

71. Dediu Newsletter, Volume 3, Number 1 (25), 6 December 2018

Mathematical research papers published in international mathematical journals

1. Dediu, M. On the lens spaces. *Rev. Roumaine Math. Pures Appl.* **14** (1969) 623-627.

2. Dediu, M. Sur quelques propriétés des espaces lenticulaires. (French) *Rev. Roumaine Math. Pures Appl.* **17** (1972), 871-874.

3. Vranceanu, G; Dediu, M. Tangent vector fields in projective spaces V_3 and in the lens spaces $L^3(3)$. (Romanian) Stud. Cerc. Mat. **24** (1972), 1585-1600.

4. Dediu, M. Tangent vector fields on lens spaces of dimension three (Italian) *Atti Accad. Naz. Lincei Rend. Cl. Sci. Fis. Mat. Natur.* **54** (1974), no. 2, 329-334 (1977

5. Dediu, M. Campi di vettori tangenti sullo spazio lenticolare $L^7(3)$. (Italian) *Atti Accad. Naz. Lincei Rend. Cl. Sci. Fis. Mat. Natur. (8)* **58** (1975), no. 1, 14-17.

6. Dediu, M. Tre campi di vettori tangenti indepedenti sugli spazi lenticolari di dimensione $4n+3$. (Italian) *Atti Accad. Naz. Lincei Rend. Cl. Sci. Fis. Mat. Natur. (8)* **58** (1975), no. 2, 174-178.

7. Dediu, M. Sopra la metrica Vranceanu generalizzata (Italian) *Atti Accad. Naz. Lincei Rend. Cl. Sci. Fis. Mat. Natur. (8)* **58** (1975), no.3, 354-359).

8. Dediu, M. Sopra la metrica Vranceanu generalizzata (Italian) *Atti Accad. Naz. Lincei Rend. Cl. Sci. Fis. Mat. Natur. (8)* **58** (1975), no.3, 354-359).

9. Dediu, S.; Dediu, M. Sopra gli spazi proiettivi. *Rend. Sem. Fac. Sci. Univ. Cagliari* **46** (1976), suppl., 149-152.

10. Dediu, M.; Caddeo, Renzo; Dediu Sofia Alcune proprietà di una superficie immersa in uno spazio di Hilbert. (Italian) *Rend. Ist. Mat. Univ. Trieste* **8** (1976), no. 2, 147-161 (1977)

11. Dediu, S.; Dediu, M.; Caddeo, R. Alcune proprietà della metrica di Vranceanu generalizzata. (Italian) *Rend Sem. Fac. Sci. Univ Cagliari* **46** (1976), suppl., 153-161.

12. Dediu, Sofia; Dediu, M.; Caddeo, Renzo The Vrănceanu metric in local coordinates. (Italian) *Atti Accad. Sci. Lett. Arti Palermo Parte I (4)* **37** (1977/78). 331-339 (1980)

13. Dediu, M.; Caddeo, Renzo; Dediu, Sofia The extension of an *E*-premanifold to an *E*-manifold. (Italian) *Rend. Circ. Mat. Palermo (2)* **27** (1978), no. 3, 353-358.

Japan: the northern side of Kawaguchiko (Lake Kawaguchi, 6 km^2, 830 m elevation), with a splendid statue (left), 17 km north of Mt. Fuji (3,776 m, 1707 last eruption), 100 km south-west of Tokyo.

Michael M. Dediu is the editor of these books (also on Amazon.com, and www.derc.com):

1. Sophia Dediu: The life and its torrents – Ana. In Europe around 1920
2. Proceedings of the 4th International Conference "Advanced Composite Materials Engineering" COMAT 2012
3. Adolf Shvedchikov: I am an eternal child of spring – poems in English, Italian, French, German, Spanish and Russian
4. Adolf Shvedchikov: Life's Enigma – poems in English, Italian and Russian
5. Adolf Shvedchikov: Everyone wants to be HAPPY – poems in English, Spanish and Russian
6. Adolf Shvedchikov: My Life, My Love – poems in English, Italian and Russian
7. Adolf Shvedchikov: I am the gardener of love – poems in English and Russian
8. Adolf Shvedchikov: Amaretta di Saronno – poems in English and Russian
9. Adolf Shvedchikov: A Russian Rediscovers America
10. Adolf Shvedchikov: Parade of Life - poems in English and Russian
11. Adolf Shvedchikov: Overcoming Sorrow - poems in English and Russian
12. Sophia Dediu: Sophia meets Japan
13. Corneliu Leu: Roosevelt, Churchill, Stalin and Hitler: Their surprising role in Eastern Europe in 1944
14. Proceedings of the 5th International Conference "Computational Mechanics and Virtual Engineering" COMEC 2013
15. Georgeta Simion – Potanga: Beyond Imagination: A Thought-provoking novel inspired from mid-20th century events
16. Ana Dediu: The poetry of my life in Europe and The USA
17. Ana Dediu: The Four Graces
18. Proceedings of the 5th International Conference "Advanced Composite Materials Engineering" COMAT 2014
19. Sophia Dediu: Chocolate Cook Book: Is there such a thing as too much chocolate?

20. Sorin Vlase: Mechanical Identifiability in Automotive Engineering

21. Gabriel Dima: The Evolution of the Aerostructures – Concept and Technologies

22. Proceedings of the 6th International Conference "Computational Mechanics and Virtual Engineering" COMEC 2015

23. Sophia Dediu: Cook Book 1 A-B-C Common sense cooking

24. Sophia Dediu: Dim Sum Spring Festival

25. Ana Dediu and Sophia Dediu: Europe in 1985: A chronological and photographic documentary

26. Stefan Staretu: Europe: Serbian Despotate of Srem and the Romanian Area – Between the 14th and the 16th Centuries

Costa Fascinosa cruise ship passing south of Piazza San Marco, Venezia, Italia, going to the Adriatic Sea.

www.ingramcontent.com/pod-product-compliance
Lightning Source LLC
Chambersburg PA
CBHW041714200326
41519CB00001B/153